MY SiDEWALKS ON
SCOTT FORESMAN
READING STREET
Intensive Reading Intervention

D1538213

Practice Book
Teacher's Manual

Level
E

PEARSON

Scott Foresman

Editorial Offices: Glenview, Illinois • Parsippany, New Jersey
New York, New York
Sales Offices: Boston, Massachusetts • Duluth, Georgia
Glenview, Illinois • Coppell, Texas • Sacramento, California • Mesa, Arizona

ISBN: 0-328-27226-4

5 6 7 8 9 10 V034 15 14 13 12 11 10 09 08 07

Contents

Vocabulary

Directions Answer the questions.

Check the Words You Know

__challenge
__chattered
__examination
__miscommunication
__misunderstand
__training
__volunteer

1. What is the prefix in the word *misunderstand*? **mis-**

2. What does the prefix in the word *misunderstand* mean? **bad or wrong**

3. What does the word *misunderstand* mean?
to not understand; to understand wrongly

4. What is the suffix in the word *examination*?
-ation

5. What does the suffix in the word *examination* mean?
being; the act of

6. What does the word *examination* mean? **being examined**

Directions Write a word from the box next to its definition.

miscommunication 7. failure to give information clearly or correctly

volunteer 8. to offer your services

chattered 9. talked constantly and quickly

examination 10. a test of knowledge or ability

misunderstand 11. to understand wrongly

challenge 12. something that tests your skill

training 13. the act of teaching a person a skill

© Pearson Education E

Home Activity This page helps your child learn to read and write vocabulary words. Work through the items with your child. Have your child use the words in items 7–13 in sentences. Check the definition to be certain your child understands the meaning of the word.

Name_____

Closed Syllables with Short Vowels

Directions Write the syllables of each word on the lines. Underline the letter in the first syllable that has a short vowel sound.

1. pilgrim _____ **p<u>i</u>l** / **grim** _____

2. hundred _____ **h<u>u</u>n** / **dred** _____

3. monster _____ **m<u>o</u>n** / **ster** _____

4. settlers _____ **s<u>e</u>t** / **tlers** _____

5. basket _____ **b<u>a</u>s** / **ket** _____

6. splendid _____ **spl<u>e</u>n** / **did** _____

Directions Circle the word that has the VCCCV syllable pattern. Then write a sentence on the line that uses the word you circled.

Sentences will vary but should include the circled words.

7. forgive (children) wonder

_____

8. human (partner) winner

_____

9. (complain) number writer

_____

10. planet (inspect) happen

_____

11. mitten rabbit (sample)

_____

12. puppets (address) copper

_____

Home Activity This page practices words with the syllable pattern found in *rub/ber* and the syllable pattern found in *mon/ster*. Read the words in items 1–6 with your child. Then invite your child to use the words in sentences.

© Pearson Education E

Name_____

Sequence

- **Sequence** is the order in which things happen in a story.
- Sometimes **clue words** can help you. They can tell you what happens first, next, and last. Some stories tell about the times or dates when things happen.

Directions Read the passage. Then answer the questions.

> Marcus was getting ready. First he put three new pencils in his backpack. Then he put his notebook in his backpack. Next, he asked his mom for some lunch money and put it in the front pocket of the backpack. Finally, he put his backpack by the front door so he could grab it as he left for the first day of school.

1. What was the first thing Marcus put in his backpack?

three pencils

2. What was the second thing Marcus put in his backpack?

his notebook

3. What was the last thing Marcus put in his backpack?

his lunch money

4. Where did Marcus finally put his backpack?

by the front door

5. For what was Marcus getting ready?

the first day of school

Home Activity This page practices identifying the sequence of events in a passage. Work through the page with your child. Then ask your child to show you how Marcus packed his backpack by acting out the steps in the story in the correct order.

Name_____

Writing

There are many kinds, or categories, of things that will help you to be successful in school. Some things that help you succeed are your school supplies. Good habits also help. You could write about just one thing or you could write about several different things. But be sure to be specific.

Directions Fill in the word webs with words and phrases from the box.

always doing homework	not talking in class
being polite	paper
pens	pencils
listening to the teacher	dictionary

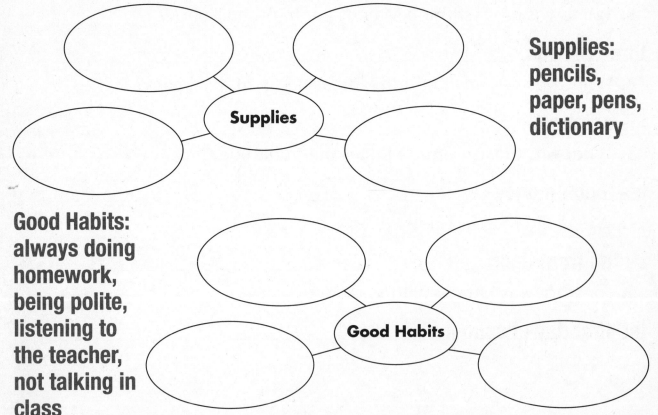

Supplies: pencils, paper, pens, dictionary

Good Habits: always doing homework, being polite, listening to the teacher, not talking in class

© Pearson Education E

What does it take to be successful in school? Write your answer on another sheet of paper. Make sure you tell why the things are important to success.

School + Home

Home Activity This page helps your child think of ways to answer the question: What does it take to be successful in school? Help your child complete each of the webs. Help your child draw and complete another word web about teachers and how they help students be successful in school.

Name_____

Vocabulary

Directions Choose the word from the box that matches each clue.
Write the word on the line.

__termite__ 1. a small insect

__damage__ 2. harm or injury that lessens usefulness

__construct__ 3. build

__survived__ 4. continued to live

__design__ 5. to plan out

__belongings__ 6. things that someone owns

__destruction__ 7. great damage

__disaster__ 8. an event that causes great suffering or loss

Directions Choose the word from the box that completes each sentence.
Write the word on the line.

9. The flood was a complete __disaster__ .

10. It caused __damage__ to all the buildings along the river.

11. Fortunately, everyone __survived__ the flood.

12. However, the __destruction__ was so great that the whole area would have to be rebuilt.

13. The mayor announced the __design__ for a new dam.

14. It would take a long time and a lot of money to __construct__ the new dam.

Home Activity This page helps your child learn to read and write vocabulary words. Work through the items with your child. Have your child write a humorous story about what happens when termites attack a doghouse. Encourage your child to use as many vocabulary words as possible.

Name _____

Closed Syllables with Long Vowel in 2nd Syllable

Directions Write the syllables of each word on the lines. Underline the letter in the second syllable that has a long vowel sound.

1. include   _____ **in** / **clude**
2. admire   _____ **ad** / **mire**
3. umpire   _____ **um** / **pire**
4. engage   _____ **en** / **gage**
5. exhale   _____ **ex** / **hale**
6. trombone   _____ **trom** / **bone**
7. surprise   _____ **sur** / **prise**
8. update   _____ **up** / **date**
9. arcade   _____ **ar** / **cade**

Directions Circle the word that correctly completes the sentence.

10. The word *reptile* has (one, (two)) syllables.

11. The sound of the letter *i* in the word *reptile* is ((long), short).

12. The final *e* in the word *reptile* is (long, (silent)).

13. The word *tadpole* has (one, (two)) syllables.

14. The sound of the letter *o* in *tadpole* is (short, (long)).

15. The final *e* in the word *tadpole* is (short, (silent)).

© Pearson Education E

Home Activity This page practices words with the syllable pattern found in the word *tadpole*. First have your child choose two words from the top of the page. Then use completed sentences 10–15 as a model and write six new sentences using those two words.

Name_____

Draw Conclusions

- A **conclusion** is a decision you make after thinking about the details in a story or an article.
- Sometimes your own experience can help you **draw conclusions.**

Directions Read the story. Then complete the chart to draw a conclusion.

Jeff and his friends were excited about the school's Spring Fling. "The Spring Fling will be a lot of fun. We're going to play baseball all day Saturday!" said Jeff. Jeff really liked to play baseball.

"If the weather is bad, the Spring Fling will be inside in the school gym. We'll get to play basketball all day Saturday," his friend Jimmy said. Jimmy really liked to play basketball. "Well, the sun will be out on Saturday," Mrs. Monroe said.

"Oh, boy!" Jeff said.

Detail
1. When will the Spring Fling take place?

on Saturday

Detail
2. What will the kids do if the weather is good?

play baseball outside

Detail
3. What will the kids do if the weather is bad?

play basketball in the gym

Detail
4. What will the weather be like on Saturday?

the sun will be out

CONCLUSION
5. Why does Jeff say, "Oh, boy!"?

because they'll be playing baseball

6. Does your conclusion make sense? Tell why.

Answers will vary: Yes, Jeff likes to play baseball.

Home Activity This page practices drawing a conclusion about a short story. Work through the page with your child. Then ask your child to change the story so that this sentence makes sense at the end: "Oh, well. I guess we'll be playing basketball on Saturday," Jeff said.

© Pearson Education E

Name_____

Writing

Think about the different kinds of scientists, firefighters, and medical workers.
They do many different things to help people before, during, and after natural disasters.

Directions Match each description with a word or phrase from the box.
Write the word or phrase on the line.

engineer	surgeon	emergency medical technician
firefighter	rescue team	Red Cross volunteer
nurse	weather forecaster	

__nurse_____ **1.** a medical worker who helps people in a hospital

__engineer_____ **2.** a scientist who shows people how to build
strong houses

__rescue team_____ **3.** a group of firefighters that looks for survivors
after a storm

__surgeon_____ **4.** a medical worker who repairs broken bones

__weather forecaster__ **5.** a scientist who warns people about stormy weather

__firefighter_____ **6.** a person who helps put out fires
__emergency medical
technician_____ **7.** a medical worker who gives emergency
medical care

__Red Cross volunteer__ **8.** a person who helps provide shelter and food for
natural disaster victims

Use the words in the box and their descriptions to answer the question: What
job or career would you choose that could help in a disaster? Write your answer
on another sheet of paper. Be sure to tell why you chose the job or career.

Home Activity This page helps your child think of ways to answer the question. Discuss the jobs and
careers in the matching activity. Then talk about what job or career your child is interested in. Ask your child
to read his or her answer aloud to you. Be sure it tells why your child chose that particular job or career.

Vocabulary

Directions Choose the word from the box that matches each definition. Write the word on the line.

flint _____ **1.** a very hard stone that makes a spark when struck against steel

wilderness _____ **2.** a region with few or no people living in it

environment _____ **3.** all the surrounding things, conditions, and influences that affect life

supplies _____ **4.** the food and equipment necessary for a trip

choices _____ **5.** alternatives or options for picking or selecting

prepared _____ **6.** ready beforehand for something

compass _____ **7.** a device for showing direction; its magnetic needle always points north

Directions Answer the questions using complete sentences. Use at least one vocabulary word in each answer. **Possible answers:**

8. How can a flint help you start a fire?

You can use the spark from a flint to start a fire.

9. How can a compass help you tell direction?

The needle on a compass always points north.

Home Activity This page helps your child learn to read and write vocabulary words. Work through the items with your child. Challenge your child to write one sentence using as many of the vocabulary words as possible, such as: To be **prepared** for a trip to the **wilderness**, you would need **supplies** like a **compass** and a **flint**.

Name_____

Plurals and Inflected Endings -s, -es, -ies

Directions Write the plural form of each word below. Remember to change the **y** to **i** before adding **-es.**

1. puppy **puppies**
2. party **parties**
3. bunny **bunnies**
4. pony **ponies**
5. supply **supplies**

6. guppy **guppies**
7. story **stories**
8. activity **activities**
9. butterfly **butterflies**
10. city **cities**

Directions Write the plural form of each word below.

11. page **pages**
12. meal **meals**
13. kind **kinds**
14. hiker **hikers**
15. box **boxes**

16. settler **settlers**
17. punch **punches**
18. worry **worries**
19. battery **batteries**
20. kiss **kisses**

 Home Activity This page practices forming the plural of words. Ask your child to look around your home and make a list of ten things. Then have your child write the plural form of each word. Work together and check spellings in a dictionary.

© Pearson Education E

Name_____

Compare and Contrast

- To **compare and contrast** means to tell how two or more things are alike and different.

- You can use a Venn diagram to **compare and contrast.**

Directions Think about what you would need to bring if you were going to take a trip to a very cold place. Then think about what you would need to bring if you were going to take a trip to a very hot place. Use the words from the box to complete the Venn diagram.

books	stocking
food	hat
baseball	swimsuit
cap	thick
mittens	socks
sandals	water

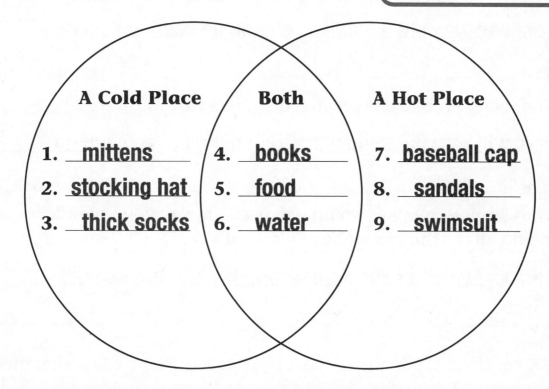

A Cold Place

1. __mittens__
2. __stocking hat__
3. __thick socks__

Both

4. __books__
5. __food__
6. __water__

A Hot Place

7. __baseball cap__
8. __sandals__
9. __swimsuit__

10. Explain why you would take some things to both a very cold place and a very hot place.

__I would need food and water no matter where I went, and books__

__could be read in both places.__

Home Activity This page practices comparing and contrasting. Work through the page with your child. Then have your child add more items to each of the three categories in the diagram. Ask your child to explain his or her choices and tell you why each one is appropriate.

Name_____

Writing

Think about the many different kinds of wilderness areas. Think about what you could do and see in each type. Decide what you would need to take with you on a trip to the area.

Directions Answer the following questions to help you gather ideas.

1. Which wilderness area would you like to visit? Circle your choice.
Choices will vary.

    Arctic   desert   forest   mountains   plains

2. On the lines below, write some words that describe the area you have chosen. Is it quiet or exciting? Cold or warm? Rainy or dry?

Answers will vary but adjectives should be used to describe the area.

3. What would you like to see and do in this wilderness area?

Answers will vary but should mention things to see and do in the area.

4. What kinds of supplies would you need to take along in order to see and do all the things you have planned?

Answers will vary but should list supplies that are needed.

On another sheet of paper, use these ideas to write about the wilderness area you would like to visit. Tell the reasons for your choice.
Answers will vary but should describe a wilderness area and include reasons for choosing the area.

Home Activity This page helps your child gather ideas and then write about a visit to a wilderness area. Work through the page with your child. Then have your child read his or her response aloud to you.

Name_____

Vocabulary

Directions Choose the word from the box that best matches each definition. Write the word on the line.

__compete__ 1. to try to win something by defeating others

__public__ 2. in view of other people

__announcer__ 3. someone who describes sporting events or reads news on radio and TV

__opponents__ 4. people on different sides in a fight, contest, or discussion

__athlete__ 5. someone trained in sports and exercises of physical strength, speed, and skill

__chance__ 6. opportunity

__conquered__ 7. successfully overcame

Directions Choose the word from the box to complete each sentence.

8. Cathy wanted to be a sports __announcer__ for her school's swim team.

9. She studied the records of each __athlete__ on the team.

10. She also studied the records of their __opponents__ at swim meets.

Home Activity This page helps your child learn to read and write vocabulary words. Work through the items with your child. Pretend that you are the radio station manager. Ask your child questions that the manager might ask at the job interview. Have your child answer using as many vocabulary words as possible.

© Pearson Education E

Verb Endings

Directions Add the endings **-ed** and **-ing** to each of the following words. Remember to double the final consonant. Write the new words on the lines.

Base Word	-ed	-ing
1. stop	stopped	stopping
2. skim	skimmed	skimming
3. bat	batted	batting
4. drop	dropped	dropping
5. plan	planned	planning

Directions Add the ending **-ed** and **-ing** to each of the following base words. Remember to drop the final **e.** Write the new words on the lines.

Base Word	-ed	-ing
6. race	raced	racing
7. hope	hoped	hoping
8. wipe	wiped	wiping
9. chase	chased	chasing
10. blame	blamed	blaming

© Pearson Education E

Home Activity This page practices verb endings with spelling changes. Work through the items on this page with your child. Then ask your child which chart the following words belong in: *score, tape, skip, scare, pat, clap.* Have him or her explain why.

Name_____

Sequence

- **Sequence** is the order in which events happen in a selection. When you read, look for clue words such as *first, next,* and *last* to help you understand the sequence of events.
- Several events can occur at the same time. Words such as *meanwhile, as,* and *during* give clues that two events are happening at the same time.

Directions Choose a word from the box to complete each sentence. Capitalize your answer if it is the first word in a sentence.

as	second
finally	then
first	third
next	when

Lu sat in the dugout mentally practicing his

swing. He pictured in his mind just how he would

hit a home run. **1.** __Then__ he heard the team manager say,

"Lu, you're on deck." Lu grabbed his glove and bat. He put his glove on

2. __as__ he walked to the deck area. **3.** __Next__

he took a few practice swings. He heard the announcer say, "At bat, Lu

Sims." He swung too high at the **4.** __first__ pitch. He swung

too late at the **5.** __second__ pitch. The **6.** __third__

pitch was a beauty. Lu smacked it hard and the ball flew over the right

field fence. The team and crowd cheered wildly. Lu loped around the

bases. **7.** __When__ he **8.** __finally__ touched home, he

thought, "Wow, practice really does make perfect!"

Home Activity This page practices using clue words that tell the sequence of events. Have your child perform a simple chore, such as emptying the wastebaskets or clearing the dishes from the dinner table. Then ask your child to tell how to do the chore using clue words to make the sequence clear. Have your child write the steps in order using clue words.

© Pearson Education E

Writing

Think about an obstacle you want to overcome. Think about the steps you would need to follow.

Directions Pretend that you want to learn to play the tuba. Write **hardest** next to the step that would be the hardest for you. Write **easiest** next to the step that would be the easiest for you. **Answers will vary.**

_____ find a tuba to practice on

_____ find a teacher

_____ have the money to pay a teacher

_____ learn to read music

Directions Pretend that you want to have a snake as a pet. Write **4** next to the step that would be the hardest for you. Write **3** next to the step that would be the next hardest. Write **1** next to the step that would be easiest for you. Write **2** next to the step that would be the next easiest. **Answers will vary.**

_____ convincing your parents that a snake would be a good pet

_____ finding a place to buy a snake

_____ taking care of a snake

_____ finding a place in your house to keep the snake

Think of a challenge you have. Make a list of the steps you would take to overcome the challenge. Put the steps in order from hardest to easiest.

School + Home

Home Activity This page helps your child understand how to put steps in a process in order from hardest to easiest. After your child writes a list of steps to overcome a personal challenge, cut the paper into strips with one step written on each strip. Help your child place the strips of paper in order, from hardest to easiest. Then ask your child to write the final list on another paper.

Name_____

Vocabulary

Directions Choose the word from the box that best matches each definition. Write the word on the line.

__population__   **1.** the people of a city, country, or district

__cultures__   **2.** lifestyles of nations or peoples of a certain time

__experience__   **3.** to have happen to you

__unexpected__   **4.** not expected; surprising

__generations__   **5.** groups of people born about the same time

__ancestry__   **6.** the people from whom you are directly descended

__discover__   **7.** to see or learn of something new

__nontraditional__   **8.** not made or done according to tradition

Check the Words You Know
__ancestry
__cultures
__discover
__experience
__generations
__nontraditional
__population
__unexpected

Directions Choose a word from the box to answer each question.

__unexpected__   **9.** What word means the opposite of *expected*?

__population__   **10.** What word means people living in a certain area?

__nontraditional__   **11.** What word means the opposite of *traditional*?

__discover__   **12.** What word means the same as *find*?

Home Activity This page helps your child learn to read and write vocabulary words. Work through the items with your child. Think of something you do or eat that you learned about from your parents, who learned about it from their parents. Share this with your child. Have your child write about it using as many vocabulary words as possible.

© Pearson Education E

Name_____

Prefixes *un-*, *dis-*, *non-*, and *re-*

Directions Add the prefix **un-**, **dis-**, **non-**, or **re-** to each base word. Write the new word on the line.

1. re + start = <u>restart</u>

2. un + clear = <u>unclear</u>

3. dis + belief = <u>disbelief</u>

4. non + fat = <u>nonfat</u>

5. dis + color = <u>discolor</u>

Directions Choose the word from the box that best fits the definition. Write the word on the line.

disarm
disconnect
dishonest
nonfiction
nonfunctional
recycle
repay
unequal
unhappy
unusual

<u>nonfiction</u> **6.** writing that deals with real people and events

<u>disarm</u> **7.** to take weapons away from

<u>unhappy</u> **8.** sad

<u>disconnect</u> **9.** to unfasten or separate

<u>repay</u> **10.** to give back; to pay back

<u>dishonest</u> **11.** showing a lack of fair play

<u>unequal</u> **12.** not the same in amount

<u>nonfunctional</u> **13.** not able to function

<u>recycle</u> **14.** to process something so it can be used again

<u>unusual</u> **15.** not ordinary; not usual

© Pearson Education E

Home Activity This page practices using the prefixes *un-*, *dis-*, *non-*, and *re-*. Work through the items with your child. Ask him or her to tell you what each prefix means. Then have your child make new words by adding one of the prefixes to the base words *fed, fill, clear, freeze, finished, stop, number,* and *wise.*

Name_____

Main Idea and Details

- The **main idea** is the most important idea about a paragraph, passage, or article.
- **Details** are small pieces of information that tell more about the main idea.

Directions Read the following passage and complete the diagram. State the main idea of the passage and three supporting details.

Bart Starr was a hero of the Green Bay Packers. He was a quarterback for the football team in the 1960s. In one game, he was able to play very well even though it was awfully windy. During another game, he was able to play very well even though it was extremely cold. With only one minute left to play, Starr threw a pass for a touchdown that won the game. Players on other teams thought that Bart Starr was the best quarterback in the league. Starr simply said, "I do the best I can."

Answers will vary. Examples are provided.

Main Idea
1. Bart Starr was a great quarterback.

Detail
2. He played a great game on an awfully windy day.

Detail
3. He played a great game on an extremely cold day.

Detail
4. Other players thought he was very good.

5. Write a one-sentence summary of this passage.

Bart Starr was a great player for the Green Bay Packers in the 1960s.

Home Activity This page practices identifying the main idea and supporting details in a brief passage. Work through the page with your child. Then have your child identify the main idea and supporting details in a short newspaper article. Challenge your child to write a summary of the article.

Name_____

Writing

Think about a country you would like to live in. Think about what you will see, hear, and do in this new country.

Directions Complete each sentence. **Answers will vary depending on the country chosen.**

1. I would like to live in _____ .

2. Before I moved to _____ , I would like to know about

   _____ .

3. If I lived in _____ , I would live in a(n)

   _____ .

4. If I lived in _____ , I would eat _____ .

5. If I lived in _____ , I would go see _____ .

6. If I lived in _____ , I would like listening to

   _____ .

7. The best thing about living in _____ would be

   _____ .

On another sheet of paper, use these ideas to write about moving to another country. Be sure to use complete sentences. Start each sentence with a capital letter and end each sentence with a punctuation mark.

Answers will vary but should include accurate information about where to live, what to eat, what to see, and what to listen to if the student lived in a different country.

Home Activity This page helps your child gather ideas and then write about moving to another country. Work through the page with your child. Encourage your child to fill in the final blanks in items 2, 3, 4, 5, and 6 with two or three things. Ask your child to read his or her paper aloud to you.

© Pearson Education E

Name_____

Vocabulary

Directions Solve each riddle using a word from the box. Write the word on the line.

Check the Words You Know

__charity
__considerate
__donate
__fortunate
__intrinsic
__organization
__support

1. I am inside someone or something.
What am I? __**intrinsic**__

2. I am as far from "unlucky" as you can get.
What am I? __**fortunate**__

3. I like to think of others—not just myself.
What am I? __**considerate**__

4. I am a group of people working together for the same purpose.
What am I? __**organization**__

5. I help the sick, the poor, and the homeless.
What am I? __**charity**__

Directions Choose the word from the box that means the same as the words in ( ). Write the word on the line.

6. Tia has been saving coins to (give away).

__**donate**__

7. Fill a Tummy is a (group that helps) that gives food to hungry people.

__**charity**__

8. Fill a Tummy needs (help).

__**support**__

9. Tia feels (lucky) that she has money to donate.

__**fortunate**__

10. Tia is (kind to) of others.

__**considerate**__

Home Activity This page helps your child read and write vocabulary words. Work through the items with your child. Then have your child make a new riddle for one of the vocabulary words. Have someone in the family try to answer the riddle.

© Pearson Education E

Name_____

Syllables with *r*-Controlled *ar, or, ore*

Directions Circle the word in each sentence that contains the same vowel sound as **ar** in **far.** Then write the word on the line.

__garden__   **1.** I have many roses in my (garden.)

__partner__   **2.** Will you be my (partner) for this game?

__carton__   **3.** Open that (carton) to find out what is inside.

__darling__   **4.** Oh, what a (darling) kitten she is!

Directions Circle the word in each sentence that contains the same vowel sound as **or** in **for** and **ore** in **more.** Then write the word on the line.

__portion__   **5.** I will have a small (portion) of that pie.

__horrible__   **6.** Please take off that (horrible) mask!

__bored__   **7.** Mel yawned and said, "I am (bored.)"

__restore__   **8.** Mr. and Mrs. Tung will (restore) that old house.

Directions In each line, circle the word that has the same vowel sound as the first word. Then underline the letters in the circled word that stand for that vowel sound.

9. park	mitten	(st<u>ar</u>dom)	finger
10. store	(ign<u>ore</u>)	party	baby
11. start	(p<u>ar</u>ticipate)	hundred	hitting
12. nor	dislike	(f<u>or</u>give)	ponies

Home Activity This page practices words with the letters *ar, or,* and *ore* with the vowel sounds heard in *partner, support,* and *restore.* Work through the page with your child. Ask your child to say an *ar* word that means "bull's-eye" *(target)* and an *or* word for "something used to lift food" *(fork).*

© Pearson Education E

Name_____

Compare and Contrast

- To **compare and contrast** means to tell how two or more things are alike and different.
- Clue words such as *like* and *as* can show similarities. Clue words such as *however* and *instead* can show differences.

Directions Read the passage. Then fill in the columns below. In the first column, write ways that Biff and Tana are alike. In the second column, write ways they are different. Some of the writing is done for you.

Biff and Tana are both Maria's pets. Biff is a dog, but Tana is a cat. Biff likes to run around and bark. Tana just likes to curl up and sleep.

Sometimes, Biff and Tana play together. They both chase the same ball. They also play tug-of-war with a string. When Tana gets tired of playing, she just sleeps.

Dinner is one thing Biff and Tana always agree on. They both love to eat! However, Biff eats dog food, while Tana eats cat food. Maria loves both her pets the same—a whole, whole lot!

Compare (Alike)	Contrast (Different)
1. **Both Biff and Tana are Maria's pets.**	4. Biff is a dog, but Tana is a cat.
2. **Biff and Tana like to play the same games.**	5. **Biff likes to run around and bark, but Tana likes to curl up and sleep.**
3. **Both Biff and Tana love to eat.**	6. **Biff eats dog food, but Tana eats cat food.**

Home Activity This page helps your child compare and contrast the two pets in the story. Ask your child to compare and contrast familiar things at home. For example, he or she could compare the kitchen with a bedroom or den.

Name_____

Writing

Think about organizing a class project to raise money. What steps would your class need to follow?

Directions The boxes below show the steps needed to get ready for the project. In each box, write a sentence to tell how your class would do that step. **The possible responses are given.**

> **1.** Decide how your class will raise money.
>
> Students will tell how their class might raise money.

↓

> **2.** Tell how the class will plan the project.
>
> They will tell how the class members will plan the project.

↓

> **3.** Tell how the class will do the work.
>
> Students will describe the work they will do to raise the money.

↓

> **4.** Tell how to collect and count the money.
>
> They will tell how the money will be collected and counted.

↓

> **5.** Tell what the charity will do with the money.
>
> Students will tell how the money will be used.

On another sheet of paper, write your description of your class project. Use the steps from this page. Make sure you use complete sentences and correct punctuation.

Home Activity This page helps your child write a description. Work through the page with your child. Then have your child read his or her description aloud.

© Pearson Education E

Name_____

Vocabulary

Directions Choose a word from the box to finish each sentence.
Write the word on the line.

<u>pose</u> **1.** I want to be a secret agent so I
can _____ as different people.

<u>beneficial</u> **2.** Studying can be _____ to
performing well in school.

<u>intervene</u> **3.** I had to _____ in the argument
between my sisters.

<u>risky</u> **4.** I think your plan to skate on
that busy street is too _____ .

<u>courageous</u> **5.** A very _____ woman pulled that child away from
a speeding car.

<u>emergency</u> **6.** We had an _____ when my brother cut his foot on
that glass.

> **Check the Words You Know**
>
> __beneficial
> __courageous
> __emergency
> __excursion
> __intervene
> __pose
> __risky

Directions Draw a line from the word to its definition.

7. beneficial   to step into or between

8. excursion   to act a part

9. courageous   full of danger

10. pose   brave

11. intervene   useful

12. risky   a quick trip for fun

Home Activity This page helps your child read and write vocabulary words. Work through the items
with your child. Then have your child look for the vocabulary words in newspapers or magazines.

© Pearson Education E

Name_____

Syllables with *r*-Controlled *er, ir, ur*

Directions Circle each word that contains the same vowel sound as **er** in **her**. Then write the word on the line.

__perky__   **1.** Let's take that (perky) puppy home!

__perfect__   **2.** I got a (perfect) score on my test.

__termite__   **3.** A (termite) is a bug that eats through wood.

__person__   **4.** The (person) who broke that window should pay for it.

Directions Circle each word that contains the same vowel sound as **ir** in **sir**. Then write the word on the line.

__dirty__   **5.** Please wash your (dirty) hands!

__circus__   **6.** I got a job in a (circus) as a clown.

__birthmark__   **7.** Zoe has a (birthmark) on her arm.

__thirsty__   **8.** If you are (thirsty,) drink some water.

Directions Circle each word that contains the same vowel sound as **ur** in **fur**. Then write the word on the line.

__purpose__   **9.** The (purpose) of this activity is to practice using commas.

__churning__   **10.** Water was (churning) at the bottom of the waterfall.

__purple__   **11.** My favorite color is (purple)

__burner__   **12.** Don't touch that hot (burner) on the stove!

Home Activity This page practices words with the vowel sounds *er* as in *certain, ir* as in *thirsty,* and *ur* as in *purple.* Work through the page with your child. Then have him or her guess words from these clues: a covering for a window (*curtain*); what a spoon can be used for (*stirring*); a word describing silver (*sterling*).

Name_____

Main Idea and Details

- The **main idea** of a story or paragraph is what it is about.
- The **details** are small pieces of information that tell something about the main idea.

Directions Read the story. Identify at least four details, and write them on the lines in the **Details** box. Then write the main idea in the **Main Idea** box.

Colors can be hot or cool. For example, people often think of green as cool. It brings to mind cool, leafy shade on a summer day. Gray is a cool color, too. It is like a cool, rainy day. Red, on the other hand, seems hot. It is like a glowing hot coal—or a spicy hot pepper. Yellow is hot, too. That's the color of the sun or of a flame burning on a candle.

Details

1. <u>Green is a cool color.</u>

_____

2. <u>Gray is a cool color.</u>

_____

3. <u>Red is a hot color.</u>

_____

4. <u>Yellow is a hot color.</u>

_____

Main Idea

5. <u>Colors can be either cool or hot.</u>

_____

 Home Activity This page helps your child state a main idea by identifying details. Work through the items with your child. Then ask your child, "How would you write about your favorite color?" Prompt your child to think of some details he or she could write.

Name_____

Writing

Think about ways to be courageous.

Directions Circle any words from the box that you might use to tell about being courageous. Write other words that you can use. Then answer the questions.

brave	emergency
strong	hero
honest	rescue
help	danger

1. <u>**Words will vary.**</u>

2. Were you ever in an emergency? What happened? What did you do?

<u>**Responses will vary depending on each student's experience.**</u>

3. Did you ever stand up for something you believe? What did you do or say? What happened?

<u>**Responses will vary.**</u>

4. Did you ever get really scared? Did you do something courageous then? Tell about it.

<u>**Responses will vary.**</u>

On another sheet of paper, write at least three sentences to tell how you could be courageous. Use one of the ideas from this page. Make sure you spell the words correctly and use correct punctuation.

Students should be able to relate to the situations even if they have not experienced them. Sentences should develop one of the situations.

© Pearson Education E

Home Activity This page helps your child write about being courageous. Work through the page with your child. Have your child read his or her own sentences aloud. Help with any necessary revising.

Vocabulary

Directions Choose a word from the box to finish each sentence. Write the word on the line shown to the left.

__panic__   **1.** Neal felt _____ when he saw the large dog running toward him.

__assistance__   **2.** That kind lady gave me _____ when I dropped coins on the floor.

__relief__   **3.** Del took medicine that gave him _____ from his sore throat.

__reunite__   **4.** Kim is eager to _____ with her family when summer camp is over.

__distress__   **5.** Jen cried out in _____ when the bee stung her.

__improve__   **6.** Your batting will _____ if you play with the team each week.

__stranded__   **7.** Leah was _____ when her bike got stuck in mud.

Write a Journal Entry

Imagine that a bad storm has struck your neighborhood. On another sheet of paper, write a journal entry describing what happened. Use as many of the vocabulary words as you can. **Answers will vary but should describe a bad storm that has struck the student's neighborhood. Some vocabulary words should be included.**

Home Activity This page helps your child read and write vocabulary words. Work through the items with your child. Then have your child tell what the vocabulary words in his or her journal entry mean.

Endings *-er*, *-est* with Multisyllabic Words

Directions Add **-er** and **-est** to each word on the left. Remember that you may have to drop the final **e** or change **y** to **i**.

Word	-er	-est
scary	scarier	scariest
1. thirsty	thirstier	thirstiest
2. gentle	gentler	gentlest
3. fluffy	fluffier	fluffiest
4. brave	braver	bravest
5. simple	simpler	simplest

Directions Add either **-er** or **-est** to the word in ( ) to complete each sentence. Write the new word on the line.

dirtier   **6.** Your shirt is (dirty) than mine.

narrower   **7.** This passage is (narrow) than that one.

funniest   **8.** That's the (funny) joke I have ever heard.

politest   **9.** Mr. Lu said I am the (polite) student in our class.

easier   **10.** I think spelling is (easy) than math.

roughest   **11.** The pilot said that was the (rough) plane ride she ever had.

littlest   **12.** That boy is holding the (little) dog I have ever seen!

Home Activity This page practices making the appropriate spelling changes when adding *-er* or *-est* to describing words. Work through the items with your child. Ask your child to use the words *silly*, *sillier*, and *silliest* in sentences and tell how each word is spelled.

© Pearson Education E

Name_____

Compare and Contrast

- When you **compare and contrast,** you tell how things are alike and different.

- Look for **clue words** that signal comparisons and contrasts, such as *like*, *both*, *different*, and *however*.

- As you read, **ask yourself,** "How are these things alike? How are they different? What do I already know about these things?"

Directions Read the story. Then complete the charts below. A sample has been done for you.

Mrs. Manos told Rita and Beth to wear shoes that would look alike for the school play. The next day, both girls wore black shoes. Their shoes had flat heels. But Rita's shoes were shiny and had bows.

Beth's shoes were canvas, and they had purple running stripes down the sides.

Mrs. Manos looked at the shoes and frowned. It was too late for the girls to change their shoes.

COMPARE

Tell how Rita's and Beth's shoes are alike.
both are black shoes
1. <u>both have flat heels</u>

CONTRAST

Rita's Shoes	Beth's Shoes
2. <u>shiny</u>	4. <u>made of canvas</u>
3. <u>have bows</u>	5. <u>have purple running stripes</u>

© Pearson Education E

Home Activity This page helps your child to compare and contrast. Work through the items with your child. Prompt him or her to think of another way shoes could be alike and another way they could be different.

Name_____

Writing

Think about a time when you helped someone and made a difference for that person.

Directions Fill in the boxes below. Then use that information to write the first sentence of your own true story about helping someone.

This is who I helped:

For items 1–4, students will provide information about their experience of helping someone, as prompted.

1. _____

This is when I helped:

2. _____

This is what I did:

3. _____

_____

This is how things turned out:

4. _____

_____

On another sheet of paper, write a paragraph about how you helped someone. Then include the information you wrote on this page plus other details. Make sure you write complete sentences.

School + Home

Home Activity This page helps your child write about an experience of helping someone. Work through the page with your child. Have your child read his or her own writing aloud.

Name_____

Vocabulary

Directions Choose the word from the box that best matches each
definition. Write the word on the line.

**Check the Words
You Know**

__aware
__conservation
__habitat
__human
__mission
__naturalists
__protect
__wildlife

__protect_____ **1.** to keep someone or
something safe from
harm or danger

__aware_____ **2.** having knowledge

__human_____ **3.** of or relating to people

__naturalists_____ **4.** scientists who study
living things

__conservation_____ **5.** protection from loss, waste, or being used up

__wildlife_____ **6.** wild animals and plants

__mission_____ **7.** purpose or goal of a group or organization

__habitat_____ **8.** where a living thing is naturally found

Directions Choose a word from the box that best matches each clue.
Write the word on the line.

__conservation_____ **9.** This refers to the care of natural resources.

__naturalists_____ **10.** These are people who know a lot about animals
and plants.

__wildlife_____ **11.** Animals and plants are examples of this.

__mission_____ **12.** This is what guides an organization.

Home Activity This page helps your child learn to read and write vocabulary words. Work through the
items with your child. Ask your child to recall a visit to a park or an afternoon in the backyard. Have your
child write about that experience using as many vocabulary words as possible.

Name_____

Open and Closed Syllables

Directions Circle each word in the box with the long vowel sound in the first syllable. Underline each word in the box with the short vowel sound in the first syllable. Then write each word in the correct column.

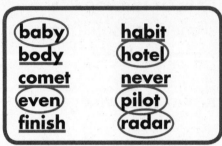

long vowel in first syllable

1. baby
2. even
3. hotel
4. pilot
5. radar

short vowel in first syllable

6. body
7. comet
8. finish
9. habit
10. never

Directions Divide each of the following words into syllables. If the vowel in the first syllable is long, check the long vowel box. If the vowel in the first syllable is short, check the short vowel box.

11. music   mu / sic   ☒ long vowel ☐ short vowel

12. tigers   ti / gers   ☒ long vowel ☐ short vowel

13. vivid   viv / id   ☐ long vowel ☒ short vowel

14. rotor   ro / tor   ☒ long vowel ☐ short vowel

15. study   stud / y   ☐ long vowel ☒ short vowel

© Pearson Education E

Home Activity This page practices words with the long and short vowel patterns in *hotel* and *never*. Ask your child to say the words in 1–10 aloud. Then have him or her divide each word into syllables. Check the syllables in a dictionary.

Draw Conclusions

- A **conclusion** is a decision you make after thinking about the details of what you read.
- Often your prior knowledge can help you draw, or make, a **conclusion.**
- When you **draw a conclusion,** be sure it makes sense and is supported by what you have read.

Directions Read the following passage. Then complete the diagram.

> Sandra loves her after-school job at the local animal shelter. She helps out three days a week and sometimes on the weekends. She usually helps feed the dogs and cats. On busy days, she also takes some of the dogs for short walks. Sandra wishes that she could take each and every dog and cat home with her. But she knows her parents would never allow that!

Detail **Possible answers:**
1. Sandra works several days a week at an animal shelter.

Detail
2. She helps feed the dogs and cats.

Detail
3. She takes the dogs for short walks.

Detail
4. She would love to take all the animals home with her.

Conclusion
5. Sandra loves animals and thinks it is important to protect them.

Home Activity This page helps your child practice drawing conclusions. Work through the page with your child. Then read a short story together and have your child draw a conclusion about one of the characters in the story.

Name_____

Writing

Think about the kind of flyer you want to make. Think about the information that will need to be included on your flyer.

Directions List ideas for a flyer describing a pet that needs an owner. Put a check mark by the things that should be included. Then write the information on the line.

☐ a picture of the pet _____

Students should include important information on their flyers and include words or pictures that will attract attention.

☐ the type of pet _____

☐ the name of the pet _____

☐ reasons someone would want a pet _____

☐ how much it costs to adopt a pet _____

☐ name of organization _____

☐ address of organization _____

☐ phone number of organization _____

☐ email address for more information _____

Use these ideas to make a flyer on another sheet of paper. The most important information should be in the largest letters. Draw something or say something on the flyer that will attract people's attention.

Home Activity This page helps your child gather ideas for preparing a flyer. Show your child flyers on the bulletin boards in stores or look at newspaper advertisements together. Discuss how the flyers or ads use pictures or big letters to attract attention. Encourage your child to do the same.

Vocabulary

Directions Choose the word from the box that best matches each definition. Write the word on the line.

__guarantee__   **1.** to promise to do something

__Constitution__   **2.** the written set of basic laws by which the United States is governed

__intolerable__   **3.** too hard or painful to bear

__battles__   **4.** fights between armies, air forces, or navies

__government__   **5.** a group of people who rule or manage a country, state, district, or city

__equality__   **6.** being equal

__freedom__   **7.** the power to do, say, or think as you please

Directions Choose the word from the box that answers each question. Write the word on the line.

__battles__   **8.** *Rights* is the plural form of the word *right*. What is the plural of *battle*?

__intolerable__   **9.** *Incorrect* has the prefix *in-*, which means "not." What word means "not able to be tolerated"?

__government__   **10.** *Enjoyment* has the suffix *-ment* and means "the act of enjoying." What word means "the act of governing"?

Home Activity This page helps your child learn to read and write vocabulary words. Work through the items with your child. Ask your child to use each of the words that are answers to items 8–12 in a sentence that shows the meaning of the word.

© Pearson Education E

Name_____

Suffixes

Directions Answer each question. Write the answers on the lines.

1. What base word and suffix do you see in *hopeful*?

__hope_____ __-ful_____

2. What base word and suffix do you see in *responsible*?

__response_____ __-ible_____

3. What base word and suffix do you see in *really*?

__real_____ __-ly_____

4. What base word and suffix do you see in *payable*?

__pay_____ __-able_____

Directions Add the suffix to each base word. Write the new word on the line.

5. perish + able = __perishable_____

6. angry + ly = __angrily_____

7. thank + ful = __thankful_____

8. defense + ible = __defensible_____

Directions Write the word from the box that best fits each definition.

__slowly_____ **9.** opposite of quickly

__collapsible_____ **10.** can be pushed together

__livable_____ **11.** fit to live in

__careful_____ **12.** opposite of careless

| careful |
| collapsible |
| livable |
| slowly |

Home Activity This page practices words that end with the suffixes *-ly, -ful, -able,* and *-ible.* Ask your child to write definitions for the new words in items 5–8. Then have him or her write sentences using the words.

Name_____

Sequence

- **Sequence** is the order in which events take place.
- Words like *then*, *after*, and *when* give clues about the order of events.

Directions Read the passage. Then fill in the time line with the events from George Washington's career. List them in the order in which they happened.

George Washington served his country in many ways. He came from Virginia to Philadelphia to help create a new country. Then he led troops during the Revolutionary War. Next, Washington returned to his home, called Mount Vernon, in Virginia. He hoped to spend his time as a farmer. However, he was soon elected President of the new nation. Washington had to leave his home once more and move to New York City. New York City was the capital of the new nation. Washington served as President of the United States for eight years. Finally, he returned once again to Mount Vernon.

George Washington's Service to the New Country

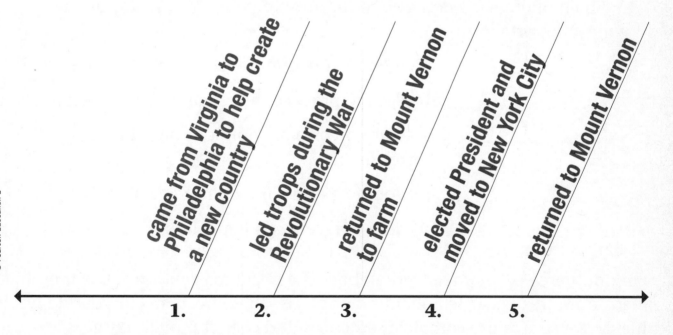

1.   2.   3.   4.   5.

Home Activity This page allows your child to identify the sequence of events using a time line. Work through the page with your child. Have your child add locations to each of the time line entries. Then ask him or her to tell about Washington's career using the information on the time line and as many sequence clue words as possible.

Name_____

Writing

Think about the freedoms you enjoy every day. How do you use these freedoms in your daily life? The questions below will help you.

Directions Answer the questions.

Answers will vary but should include an understanding of freedoms enjoyed in the student's daily life.

1. What freedoms do you have at home?

   I have the freedom to _____ on the weekends.

   I have the freedom to stay up until _____ o'clock on weekend nights.

   I have the freedom to play _____ .

2. What freedoms do you have at school?

   I have the freedom to _____ at recess.

   I have the freedom to _____ during lunch.

   I have the freedom to _____ during class.

3. Which of these freedoms are important to you? Draw a star by the most important ones.

   _____ freedom to vote after reaching 18 years old

   _____ freedom to practice the religion of my choice

   _____ freedom to voice my opinions about my government

   _____ freedom to express my opinions in writing

   _____ freedom to receive an education

On another sheet of paper, write about the freedoms you have. Use the ideas from this page. Tell about how you use these freedoms in your daily life. Make sure to use complete sentences and correct punctuation.

Home Activity This page helps your child write about freedoms. Work through the page with your child. Discuss the freedoms we have in the United States. Compare the freedoms that are most important to you as an adult with the freedoms that are most important to your child.

Name_____

Vocabulary

Directions Choose the word from the box that best matches each definition. Write the word on the line.

__theory__ **1.** an idea that explains something

__consider__ **2.** to think about in order to decide

__experiment__ **3.** a test to find out something

__brainstorm__ **4.** to think of different ways to solve a problem

__brilliant__ **5.** having a great mind filled with many ideas

__evaluate__ **6.** to find out the worth of something

__invention__ **7.** something new that has been created

__process__ **8.** a set of actions or steps

Directions Choose a word from the box to complete each sentence. Write the word on the line.

9. The light bulb was an important __invention__ .

10. Editing is a step in the writing __process__ .

11. We will perform a(n) __experiment__ in science lab today.

12. The teacher will __evaluate__ our book reports.

© Pearson Education E

Home Activity This page helps your child learn to read and write vocabulary words. Review the definitions of the vocabulary words with your child and ask him or her to use the words in sentences.

Long *a* Spelled *ai, ay*

Directions Add the first syllable to the second syllable. Write the word on the line. Underline the letters that spell the long *a* sound.

1. dis + play = __dis**pl**ay__
2. com + plain = __com**plain**__
3. ob + tain = __ob**tai**n__
4. de + cay = __de**cay**__
5. ex + claim = __ex**clai**m__

Directions Choose a word from the box to complete each sentence. Write the word on the line.

6. The game started late because of a rain __delay__ .

7. When you __remain__ still, you do not move.

8. You can support the main idea of your story with __details__ .

9. How far __away__ from the road is the river?

10. Can you __explain__ how to make this dish?

away
delay
details
explain
remain

Directions Circle the word in each group that has the same vowel sound as **way**.

11. (retail)   tapped   relax
12. basket   (essay)   sadly
13. tadpole   (proclaim)   happy
14. (contain)   happy   gallon

Home Activity This page practices words with long *a* spelled *ai* and *ay*. Work through the items with your child. Then give your child five minutes to list words with the long *a* sound spelled *ai* and *ay*.

Name _____

Sequence

- **Sequence** is the order in which events take place.
- Words such as *first, then, after,* and *later* give clues about the order of events.

Directions Read the passage. Then complete the diagram.

My sister and I are going to make a small house for our dog, Ronny. First, we will study the detailed plans. Next, we will buy supplies such as wood, nails, and paint.

After we have the things we need, we will start building the house. Then we will paint it. Later, when the paint is dry, we will let Ronny sleep in his new house!

Step 1
Study the plans for the house.

↓

Step 2
Buy some wood, nails, and paint.

↓

Step 3
Start building the house.

↓

Step 4
Paint the new house.

↓

Step 5
Let the dog sleep in the house.

 Home Activity This page allows your child to identify sequence of events. Work through the page with your child. Then tell your child how to make a simple breakfast dish. Have your child retell the steps in the process in the correct order.

Name_____

Writing

Think about what you would like to invent. Do you want to invent something that helps you do your chores? Would your invention help you do your homework? Would it be something that helps your mom or your dad do their work? Or would it be something that helps animals?

Directions Fill in the blanks. **Answers will vary.**

1. I want to invent _____.

2. I will name my invention _____.

Directions Complete the diagram to show the steps you would follow in making your invention.

```
┌─────────────────────────────────────────────────────────────┐
│                    Sequence of Events                        │
│  1. Students should identify sequential steps for making their invention. │
└─────────────────────────────────────────────────────────────┘
                              ↓
┌─────────────────────────────────────────────────────────────┐
│  2.                                                          │
└─────────────────────────────────────────────────────────────┘
                              ↓
┌─────────────────────────────────────────────────────────────┐
│  3.                                                          │
└─────────────────────────────────────────────────────────────┘
                              ↓
┌─────────────────────────────────────────────────────────────┐
│  4.                                                          │
└─────────────────────────────────────────────────────────────┘
```

On another sheet of paper, write about the steps you would take to create your invention.
Answers should include ordered steps from idea to completed invention.

Home Activity This page helps your child name steps for making an invention. Work through the page with your child. Then cut the page apart so that each step is on one strip of paper. Mix the steps and have your child reorder them.

Name_____

Vocabulary

Directions Choose the word from the box that best matches each definition. Write the word on the line.

__collections___ **1.** groups of items, such as works of art

__mural___ **2.** picture painted on a wall

__famous___ **3.** very well-known

__canvas___ **4.** a strong cloth that is painted on

__styles___ **5.** ways of painting, writing, composing, or building

__gallery___ **6.** place where art is displayed

__express___ **7.** to show through words, looks, or actions

Directions Choose a word from the box that matches each clue. Write the word on the line.

8. Many students helped paint the colorful __mural___ on the wall of the school.

9. The well-known works of many __famous___ artists, including Grant Wood, are on display that museum.

10. My mom had the picture I painted on __canvas___ framed.

11. That museum has __collections___ of folk and modern art on display.

12. That __gallery___ has art shows displaying the works of local artists.

Home Activity This page helps your child learn to read and write vocabulary words. Work through the page with your child. Ask your child to plan a mural and tell what it would show.

Long e Spelled e, ee, ea

Directions Underline the letter or letters in the following words that make the long e sound. Write the words on the line.

__exceed_____ 1. exc<u>ee</u>d

__eager_____ 2. <u>e</u>ager

__fever_____ 3. f<u>e</u>ver

__asleep_____ 4. asl<u>ee</u>p

__appeal_____ 5. app<u>ea</u>l

__relay_____ 6. r<u>e</u>lay

Directions Put the words in the chart to match the spelling pattern of the long e sound.

| conceal | rebate | proceed | freedom | weaken |
| prefix | fifteen | rebus | reason | |

long e spelled e	long e spelled ea	long e spelled ee
7. **prefix**	10. **conceal**	13. **fifteen**
8. **rebate**	11. **reason**	14. **freedom**
9. **rebus**	12. **weaken**	15. **proceed**

Directions Circle the word in each pair that has the long e sound spelled ea.

16. heavy (treaty) 17.(reveal) sweater 18.(season) feather

Home Activity This page practices words that have syllables with the long e sound spelled e, ee, or ea as in *fever, exceed,* and *appeal.* Work through the items with your child. Then ask your child to make a list of words with the long e sound spelled e, ee, and ea.

© Pearson Education E

Name_____

Main Idea

- The **main idea** is the most important idea about a paragraph, passage, or article.
- **Details** are small pieces of information that tell more about the main idea.

Directions Read the following passage and complete the diagram. State the main idea of the passage and three supporting details.

Our class saw many things from the past on our field trip to the museum. We saw mummies in one display. We saw bones of big animals such as mammoths. We saw insects in amber. We saw jars and baskets made by people long ago. We even saw an old car. Our teacher said it was one of the first cars made. We had a good time learning about things from the past at the museum.

Main Idea

1. **Our class saw many things from the past on our field trip to the museum.**

Accept any of these details:

Supporting Details

2. **We saw mummies in one display. We saw bones of big animals such as mammoths.**

3. **We saw insects in amber. We saw jars and baskets made by people long ago.**

4. **We even saw an old car. Our teacher said it was one of the first cars made.**

© Pearson Education E

School + Home

Home Activity This page allows your child to identify main idea and supporting details. Work through the page with your child. Help your child identify the main idea and supporting details for several paragraphs in a newspaper.

Name_____

Writing

Think about the art projects you have done. What did you use to complete the project? Which project was the most fun to do?

Directions Use the web below to list art project ideas. They can be projects you have done or projects you might like to do. You can add more kinds of art projects to the web if you like. Then draw a star by the idea you like best.

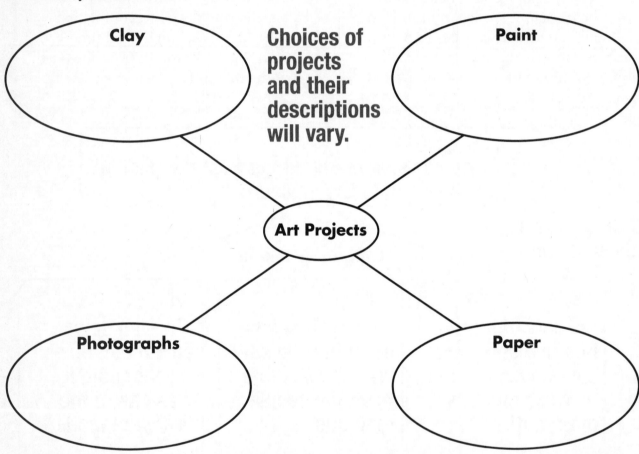

Clay

Choices of projects and their descriptions will vary.

Paint

Art Projects

Photographs

Paper

On another sheet of paper, describe the art project and tell why you like it. Tell about the supplies you will use to complete the project and how the finished project will look. Be sure to use complete sentences and to spell words correctly.

Answers will vary but should include visual descriptions.

Home Activity This page helps your child describe an art project. Work through the page with your child. Ask your child to tell you about his or her second choice for a favorite art project.

48 Writing

Practice Book Unit 3

© Pearson Education E

Name_____

Vocabulary

Directions Choose the word from the box that matches each definition. Write the word on the line.

<u>extinct</u>   **1.** no longer existing

<u>prehistoric</u>   **2.** of or belonging to times before histories were written

<u>paleontologists</u>   **3.** scientists who study the forms of life that lived long ago

<u>excavated</u>   **4.** dug out and removed from a site

<u>sites</u>   **5.** places where things are located

<u>sandstone</u>   **6.** a kind of rock made mostly of sand

<u>fossils</u>   **7.** hardened remains or prints of plants or animals that lived long ago

> ### Check the Words You Know
>
> __excavated
> __extinct
> __fossils
> __paleontologists
> __prehistoric
> __sandstone
> __sites

Directions Choose a word from the box that best completes each sentence. Write the word on the line.

8. Mammoths are one kind of animal that <u>**paleontologists**</u> have studied.

9. The <u>**fossils**</u>, or remains, of mammoths have been found in many places.

10. Workers might have used hammers and chisels as they <u>**excavated**</u>, or dug up, fossils of mammoths.

© Pearson Education E

 School + Home **Home Activity** This page helps your child learn to read and write vocabulary words. Work through the page with your child. Ask your child to tell you about mammoths. Encourage him or her to use as many vocabulary words as possible.

Name_____

Contractions

- A **contraction** is a shortened form of a word or group of words.
- In a **contraction,** an apostrophe takes the place of the letters that have been removed.

Directions Use each pair of words to make a contraction. Write the contraction on the line.

__didn't__ **1.** did not   __aren't__ **6.** are not

__it's__ **2.** it is   __they're__ **7.** they are

__here's__ **3.** here is   __they've__ **8.** they have

__what's__ **4.** what is   __shouldn't__ **9.** should not

__let's__ **5.** let us   __isn't__ **10.** is not

Directions Draw a line to match each set of words to its contraction.

11. she will   they'll

12. they will   won't

13. do not   don't

14. will not   she'll

Directions Make a contraction of the words in ( ) to complete each sentence. Write the contraction on the line.

__I'm__ **15.** (I am) hoping to become a fossil hunter.

__haven't__ **16.** Fossils (have not) been found at this site yet.

__can't__ **17.** He (cannot) tell what kind of bone this is.

__isn't__ **18.** It (is not) a mammoth bone.

Home Activity This page practices contractions. Ask your child to make as many contractions as he or she can from these words: *here, they, he, is, are, will, have.*

© Pearson Education E

50 **Phonics** Contractions   **Practice Book Unit 3**

Name _____

Draw Conclusions

- A **conclusion** is a decision you make after thinking about the details of what you read.
- Often your prior knowledge can help you draw, or make, conclusions.
- When you draw a conclusion, be sure it makes sense and is supported by what you have read.

Directions Read the following passage. Then complete the diagram.

Cliff's mother called to him as he was getting ready for school. "I have to help your sister. Will you finish up in the kitchen for me?" she asked. Cliff went into the kitchen. He saw a loaf of bread, slices of cheese, and a head of lettuce. There were also two small bags of carrots and two drink boxes. Next to the drink boxes were lunch bags. "Well, now I know what my mom wanted me to do," Cliff said.

Conclusion:
5. Cliff is supposed to make the sandwiches and pack lunches.

Possible responses:

Supporting Details

Detail:
1. Cliff went to the kitchen.

Detail:
2. His mom had set out bread, cheese, and lettuce.

Detail:
3. Cliff found lunch bags in the kitchen.

What you know:
4. Some kids pack lunches to take to school.

© Pearson Education E

School + Home **Home Activity** This page allows your child to draw a conclusion from facts or details in a reading passage. Tell your child about an event that happened in your life. Have your child single out two or three details from the story and draw a conclusion about it.

Name_____

Writing

Think about what you know about animal fossils. Imagine you are a fossil hunter and have found the bones or other remains of an extinct animal. It can be a real or an imaginary animal.

Directions Answer the questions to help describe the fossil remains you found.
Descriptions should include the animal's name and characteristics.

1. What animal did you find? What is it named?

_____

2. How heavy was your animal?

_____

3. How long was your animal?

_____

4. What did your animal eat—plants or animals or both? Tell what kinds of things it ate.

_____

5. Where did your animal live?

_____

6. How did your animal move around?

_____

7. What did your animal look like? Did it have feet? Did it have wings or fins? Did it have feathers or fur or scales? Did it have a tail?

_____

On another sheet of paper, write about the animal you found. Tell its name. Tell what it looked like. Tell what it did.

Home Activity This page helps your child use his or her imagination to write a description of an animal whose fossil has been found. Work through the page with your child. Help your child make a drawing of the animal to go with the description.

© Pearson Education E

Name_____

Vocabulary

Directions Choose the word from the box that best matches each definition. Write the word on the line.

___fiddle_____ **1.** a kind of violin

___instrument_____ **2.** a device for making music

___beat_____ **3.** the unit of time in music

___studio_____ **4.** a place where music is made and copied

___harmony_____ **5.** the blending together of the sounds of music

___record_____ **6.** to copy music, words, or pictures for later use

___concert_____ **7.** a public performance of music

Directions Many words have more than one meaning. Read the pairs of sentences. Put a check mark by the sentence in which the vocabulary word has the definition listed above.

8. _____ The police officer walks a *beat* every day.

  ✓ The dancers moved to the *beat* of the drums.

9. _____ That is one *instrument* a dentist uses to clean teeth.

  ✓ What *instrument* do you play in the marching band?

10. ✓ The *harmony* of singing voices was beautiful to listen to.

  _____ The neighbors worked in *harmony* to build the stone wall.

Home Activity This page helps your child learn to read and write vocabulary words. Work through the page with your child. Then ask your child to use the vocabulary words as he or she explains the choices made for items 8–10.

Name_____

Long *o* Spelled *oa, ow*

Directions Choose a word from the box that rhymes with each word.
Write the word on the line.

road
fellow
borrow
toasted

___toasted___   **1.** roasted

___fellow___   **2.** yellow

___borrow___   **3.** sorrow

___road___   **4.** load

Directions Circle the word in each group that has a long *o* sound.
Then write the word on the line.

___charcoal___   **5.** bottom   (charcoal)   progress

___hollow___   **6.** (hollow)   border   contract

___approach___   **7.** proper   rocket   (approach)

___railroad___   **8.** novel   inform   (railroad)

Directions Write the word that has the long *o* sound on the line.
Then underline the letters that make the long *o* sound.

___shad<u>ow</u>___   **9.** A shadow forms when light is blocked.

___rainc<u>oa</u>t___   **10.** I wore a raincoat to keep dry.

___s<u>oa</u>king___   **11.** Rob got soaking wet during the storm.

___wind<u>ow</u>s___   **12.** We shut all the windows before the storm hit.

Home Activity This page practices words with the long *o* sound spelled *oa* or *ow*. Have your child choose words from the activities with the long *o* sound and use them in sentences.

Name_____

Main Idea

- The **main idea** is what a story is all about.
- **Details** are small pieces of information that help tell more about the story.

Directions Read the following passage. Then answer the questions.

> Robert loves planes and flying. One of the things he likes to do best is watch planes take off and land. He likes to watch planes approach the landing strip. He watches as they speed down the runway for takeoff. He has flown with his parents many times. Robert plans to take flying lessons. He hopes to become a pilot.

1. What is the topic of the passage?

<u>Robert loves planes and flying.</u>

Name four details that support the main idea. **Possible details:**

2. <u>He likes to watch planes take off and land.</u>

3. <u>He likes to watch planes approach the landing strip.</u>

4. <u>He watches as they speed down the runway for takeoff.</u>

5. <u>He has flown with his parents many times.</u>

6. Write a summary of the passage in one or two sentences.

<u>Robert loves planes and flying and hopes to become a pilot.</u>

_____

_____

Home Activity This page allows your child to read a short passage and identify its main idea and supporting details. Read a short newspaper or magazine article with your child and have him or her identify its main idea and supporting details.

Name_____

Writing

Directions Read the information and complete the lists.

1. You strike a drum to make music. You can make drums and drumsticks with things you have at home. List things you have at home that could be used as drumsticks, such as rulers, and drums, such as empty cans with plastic lids.

Ideas for Drums and Drumsticks

<u>Lists will vary. Students should provide step-by-step</u>

<u>directions for making their instrument.</u>

2. You can blow into some instruments, such as a horn, to make music. Make a list of things that could be used as a wind instrument, such as a cardboard tube from a roll of paper towels.

Ideas for Wind Instruments

_____   _____

_____   _____

3. You can pluck or pull the strings of some instruments, such as fiddles, to make music. Make a list of things that could be used to make a stringed instrument, such as rubber bands stretched over a bowl.

Ideas for Stringed Instruments

_____   _____

_____   _____

On another sheet of paper, write a description of the instrument you will make. Tell how to make it and how to play it.

Home Activity This page helps your child develop ideas for making a homemade musical instrument. Ask your child to tell you how to make an instrument and follow his or her directions. You can then play your instruments together.

© Pearson Education E

Name_____

Vocabulary

Directions Choose the word from the box that best matches each definition. Write the word on the line.

__theater__   **1.** a place where plays are acted or movies are shown

__illusions__   **2.** things that appear to be different from what they actually are

__live__   **3.** presented at the time it is happening; not recorded

__audience__   **4.** people gathered to see or hear something

__effects__   **5.** things that produce impressions on the mind or senses

__broadcast__   **6.** a radio or television program

__performers__   **7.** people who entertain others

Directions Choose a word from the box to complete each sentence. Write the word on the line.

__live__   **8.** That band performed _____ at a concert.

__illusions__   **9.** The magician uses _____ to trick our eyes.

__effects__   **10.** Many special _____ are used in movies today.

__theater__   **11.** We went to the _____ to see a play.

__performers__   **12.** The actors on stage are also called _____ .

Home Activity This page helps your child read and write vocabulary words. With your child, listen to a radio or television commercial. Ask your child to tell about what he or she heard. Encourage your child to use as many vocabulary words as possible.

© Pearson Education E

Name_____

Prefixes *in-, im-, il-, ir-*

Directions Choose a word from the box to match each definition. Write the word on the line. Then, circle the word's prefix that means "not."

illegible	imbalance	impassable	impolite	impossible
inactive	incomplete	insecure	irregular	irresponsible

(**im**)polite _____ **1.** not having good manners

(**il**)legible _____ **2.** not legible; not easy to read

(**im**)possible _____ **3.** not capable of being done

(**in**)complete _____ **4.** not finished

(**in**)secure _____ **5.** not safe from danger

(**ir**)responsible _____ **6.** not responsible

(**im**)balance _____ **7.** not in balance

(**ir**)regular _____ **8.** not regular

(**in**)active _____ **9.** not moving

(**im**)passable _____ **10.** not able to be traveled over

Directions Add the prefix to the base word to make a new word. Write the new word on the line. Then, write a definition for the new word.

11. ir + replaceable   **irreplaceable** : **not replaceable**

12. in + direct   **indirect** : **not direct**

13. im + perfect   **imperfect** : **not perfect**

© Pearson Education E

Home Activity This page practices words with the prefixes *in-, im-, il-* and *ir-*, which mean "not." Help your child use the prefixes with the following base words: *mature (immature), logical (illogical), resistible (irresistible), sensitive (insensitive)*. Together use a dictionary to define the new words.

Name_____

Compare and Contrast

- To **compare and contrast** means to tell how two or more things are alike and different.

Directions Read the passage below. Then complete the Venn diagram by comparing and contrasting the two bikes.

Today I am going with a friend to shop for a new bike. The bike I own is very old and I want a new one. My old bike is very heavy. This means I have to pedal very hard to gain speed. My new bike will not be heavy at all. It will be much easier to ride. But I plan on getting a red bike—just like my old bike!

Old Bike

The bike is old. The bike is heavy. It must be pedaled hard to gain speed.

Both Bikes

The bikes are red.

New Bike

The bike is new. The bike is not heavy. It will be easier to ride than the old bike.

Home Activity This page allows your child to tell how two bikes are alike and different. Choose two pictures from a magazine that are of people, animals, or plants. Ask your child to explain how the two pictures are alike and different.

Name_____

Writing

Think about how masks are used by actors. Masks can make an old actor look young. Masks can make an actor look like an animal. Masks can make an actor look like a creature from outer space. Masks can simply hide a character's face so the other characters don't know who it is.

Directions Draw a mask in the box below. Then complete the sentences.

1. My mask shows a face like _____ .

2. My mask could be made from _____ .

3. An actor would wear my mask to _____ .

4. My mask could be used to _____ .

Use the information in the sentences to write a description of your mask. Tell what makes your mask special. Be sure that all the words in your description are spelled correctly.

Descriptions will depend on the kinds of masks students draw.

© Pearson Education E

Home Activity This page helps your child gather ideas for designing a mask. Encourage your child to look at the pictures in storybooks or magazines to get ideas for details to add to the drawing of the mask.

Name_____

Vocabulary

Directions Choose the word from the box that matches each clue.
Write the word on the line.

salvage   **1.** to save from being destroyed

suburban   **2.** of or in an area outside a city

potential   **3.** something that may be
possible as time goes on

property   **4.** land owned by someone

reuse   **5.** to use again

urban   **6.** of or in a city or a town

congestion   **7.** overcrowded condition

rural   **8.** of or in the country

> **Check the Words
> You Know**
>
> __congestion
> __potential
> __property
> __reuse
> __rural
> __salvage
> __suburban
> __urban

Directions Choose the word from the box that best completes each
sentence. Write the word on the line.

Janelle doesn't like the **9.** **_congestion_** of the city. It's much too

crowded for her. That's why she moved to a **10.** **_suburban_**

area on the city's edge. Now, this area is becoming crowded, too. Janelle

may soon move out to a(n) **11.** **_rural_** area. Will, however,

is a city person. He doesn't want to live anywhere except in a(n)

12. **_urban_** area.

Home Activity This page helps your child read and write vocabulary words. Work through the items with
your child. Have your child make up his or her own clue for one of the vocabulary words.

© Pearson Education E

Name_____

Compound Words

Directions Combine each pair of words to make a compound word. Write the new word on the line.

1. some + where = __somewhere__

2. club + house = __clubhouse__

3. thunder + storm = __thunderstorm__

4. drive + way = __driveway__

5. any + one = __anyone__

6. drum + stick = __drumstick__

7. sweat + shirt = __sweatshirt__

Directions Write the compound word from the box that matches the underlined words.

	boxcar
	homework
	storefront
	classroom
	fireplace

__storefront__   8. Look in the <u>front of the shop</u> to see what they are selling.

__fireplace__   9. In winter, I love having a <u>place to burn wood.</u>

__classroom__   10. We walked back to the <u>room where class is held</u> to see if I left the book there.

__homework__   11. Maya did some of her <u>studying to be completed outside of class</u> in study hall.

__boxcar__   12. The workers will unload the <u>closed-in car of the train.</u>

School + Home **Home Activity** This page practices compound words. Work through the items with your child. Ask your child to make as many compound words as he or she can with the words *house* and *boat*.

Name_____

Draw Conclusions

- A **conclusion** is a decision you reach based on what you read and what you know.
- Use **facts** and **details** to help you draw a conclusion.

Directions Read the story. Then answer the questions. Use your answers to form and write your own conclusion.

"Everyone loves summer!" said Sandy.

"Not me," said Nat. "It's too hot. I like fall the best."

"You're both wrong," said Inez. "Spring is the best season. The trees and other plants are so beautiful then."

"Excuse me," said Josh. "I think winter is best. It's fun to curl up by the fire with something to read."

"You've got to be kidding!" said the others.

"No, I'm not!" said Josh. Soon other kids chimed in with their ideas about the best season. And some even agreed with Josh.

1. What season does Nat like best? __**fall**__

2. What season does Inez like best? __**spring**__

3. What season does Josh like best? __**winter**__

4. What season do you like best? __**Students should write one of the four seasons.**__

5. Now think about the story and the answers you wrote. You can draw conclusions from these facts and what you know. Write your conclusion in a complete sentence on the lines.

Possible conclusions: People don't all like the same season; People have different favorite seasons; People don't all agree on their favorite season.

© Pearson Education E

Home Activity This page allows your child to draw a conclusion. Work through the items with your child. Then talk about your favorite season without naming it. Have your child use the information to draw conclusions about your favorite season.

Name_____

Writing

Think about writing a description of how to use a schoolroom. First think of the different ways in which rooms are usually used.

Directions Read the list of schoolrooms. Then choose one room you'd like to change. Put a check mark beside it.

> __**library**   used for getting books and studying
> __**auditorium**   used to put on programs for large groups
> __**sports room**   used for playing sports
> __**classroom**   used for teaching and learning
> __**lunchroom**   used for eating lunch
> __**office**   used by the principal to run the school
> __**music room**   used for music classes
> __**entry hall**   used by people coming into the school

Now think of another way to use the room you chose. Think about details you would change so that it can be used in the new way. Some examples of details are desks, tables, cabinets, shelves, machines, and colors. Answer the questions below.

  1. How would you use the room? Write a complete sentence.

<u>**Students' descriptions should identify the rooms and how they must**</u>

<u>**be adapted for the new use.**</u>

  2. What would you change in the room?

<u>**Responses will vary.**</u>

On another paper, write your description. Your writing should help readers "see" the changes you want to make to the room.

Home Activity This page helps your child write a description. Work through the page with your child. Have your child read the description aloud.

Vocabulary

Directions Choose the word from the box that matches each clue.
Write the word on the line.

___persist___ **1.** If you keep trying and trying, you do this.

___successful___ **2.** If a party you planned turned out well, it was this.

___rehabilitation___ **3.** If someone needs to restore health, he or she may need this.

___physical___ **4.** If you are doing pushups, you are doing this kind of exercise.

___dyslexia___ **5.** If you find it difficult to read, you may need to be checked for this.

___adapt___ **6.** Some animals can do this by changing color to match something where they live.

___confidently___ **7.** If you're sure of yourself, you do things this way.

> **Check the Words You Know**
> __adapt
> __confidently
> __dyslexia
> __persist
> __physical
> __rehabilitation
> __successful

Directions Choose a word from the box that fits the meaning of the sentence. Write the word on the line.

8. Emily's attempt to make a free throw was ___successful___ .

9. Dan walked to the stage ___confidently___ and began singing.

10. All the teams have to ___adapt___ to the changes in the rules.

11. People with ___dyslexia___ work very hard to build reading skills.

12. Instead of giving up, you should ___persist___ and try to win.

Home Activity This page helps your child read and write vocabulary words. Work through the items with your child. Then have your child use the vocabulary words to write a newspaper article.

© Pearson Education E

Name_____

Long *i* Spelled *igh*, *ie*, Final *y*

Directions Circle each word that has long *i* spelled **igh**. Then write the word on the line.

delighted   **1.** Calvin was (delighted) to meet a tennis star.

lightning   **2.** (Lightning) flashed across the sky.

frightened   **3.** Many people are (frightened) of snakes.

insights   **4.** Reading that book gave me (insights) into how people lived long ago.

Directions Circle each word that contains the long *i* sound spelled **ie.** Then write the word on the line.

relies   **5.** Mom (relies) on my brother and me to help her.

applied   **6.** Has anyone (applied) for the job yet?

classified   **7.** We (classified) the objects in three different ways.

supplies   **8.** We went to the store to get school (supplies).

Directions Circle each word that contains the same vowel sound as **y** in **fly**. Then write the word on the line.

satisfy   **9.** A big glass of water will (satisfy) my thirst.

python   **10.** A (python) is a large snake.

reply   **11.** Did you get a (reply) to your letter?

multiply   **12.** You (multiply) to find the product of two numbers.

© Pearson Education E

Home Activity This page practices words that spell long *i* as *igh*, *ie*, or *y*. Work through the items with your child. Ask your child to write sentences using each of these words: *insights, allies, deny.*

Name_____

Compare and Contrast

- To **compare and contrast** means to tell how two or more things are alike and different.

Directions Read the ad for Zip pens. Then follow the directions to compare and contrast the pens.

> Which pen is right for you? The Zip 5 is a great pen with a bold look. It is wide and easy to grip. Choose a Zip 5 with pink, green, or red ink. You can always find this pen because it glows in the dark. The Zip 10 is a pen for real work, such as writing test answers. It is thin and sleek and has a clip. You can clip it to a notepad or on the strap of your backpack. The Zip 10 comes in either black or blue ink. Both Zip pens last at least a year. And both will work even if they get wet!

Directions: Answer the questions.

How are the Zip pens alike? Write two ways.

1. **Possible responses: last one year; work even when wet;** _____

_____

2. **made by the same company, have ink** _____

_____

How is the Zip 5 pen not like Zip 10? Write two ways.

3. **Possible responses: is wide and easy to grip;** _____

_____

4. **has pink, green, or red ink; glows in the dark** _____

_____

Home Activity This page helps your child compare and contrast. Work through the items with your child. Then choose two similar household objects and have your child tell how they are the same and different.

Name_____

Writing

Humans have five senses—sight, smell, taste, hearing, and touch. Think how you use your senses to find out about the world around you.

Directions: Each description below tells about using one of the five senses. Read the description. Then write the sense it uses on the line.

taste   **1.** You bite into a crisp apple.

hearing   **2.** You enjoy the music played by the school band.

sight   **3.** You watch a mime perform on stage.

touch   **4.** You pet your puppy asleep on your lap.

smell   **5.** You get a whiff of bread baking in the oven.

Choose one of the senses. List ways that you use the sense every day.

Responses will vary depending on student's choice.

_____

_____

On another sheet, write a paragraph that tells why that sense is important to you. Include details that explain your choice.

Students should choose one of the senses and explain why it is important. They should support their choice with details. For example, if they choose smell, they might state that it enables them to detect dangerous odors, such as gas, as well as enjoy pleasant aromas.

© Pearson Education E

Name_____

Vocabulary

Directions Choose a word from the box that best fits the meaning of the sentence. Write the word on the line.

Check the Words You Know

__adopt
__camouflage
__domestic
__feral
__nurture
__tame
__transform

1. The cowboy tried to __**tame**__ that wild horse.

2. A coat of paint will __**transform**__ my room.

3. A mother cat knows how to __**nurture**__ her kittens.

4. We can __**adopt**__ a puppy from the animal shelter.

5. Cows and sheep are examples of __**domestic**__ animals raised on farms and ranches.

6. The snowshoe hare's white fur is its __**camouflage**__ in winter.

7. These __**feral**__ cats became wild after living on their own in the forest.

Directions Draw a line from the word to its definition.

8. adopt   returned to wildness

9. transform   to care for

10. nurture   to change greatly

11. camouflage   a look that lets something blend in with things around it

12. feral   to take in a child or an animal as one's own

Write a Letter

Imagine taking a trip to a farm. Write a letter to a friend about it. Use as many vocabulary words as you can. **Answers will vary.**

Home Activity This page helps your child read and write vocabulary words. Work through the items with your child. Encourage him or her to write about some animals in the letter.

Consonant + *le* Syllables

Directions Write the two syllables that make up each word on the lines.

1. __ta__ + __ble__ = table

2. __gob__ + __ble__ = gobble

3. __a__ + __ble__ = able

4. __sin__ + __gle__ = single

5. __gig__ + __gle__ = giggle

6. __ca__ + __ble__ = cable

7. __sam__ + __ple__ = sample

8. __ti__ + __tle__ = title

9. __sprin__ + __kle__ = sprinkle

10. __cir__ + __cle__ = circle

Directions Choose the word in the box that matches each clue. Write the word on the line. Then draw a line to divide it into its syllables.

| bugle | fable | fumble | nibble | simple |

11. to take tiny bites __nib / ble__

12. easy to do or understand __sim / ple__

13. to juggle and drop __fum / ble__

14. a horn like a trumpet __bu / gle__

15. a story that teaches a lesson __fa / ble__

Home Activity This page practices words ending in a syllable with consonant plus *le*. Work through the items with your child. Ask your child to think of two other words with this pattern.

Name_____

Sequence

- **Sequence** is the order in which things happen in a story.
- **Clue words**, such as *first, now, then, a month ago, as,* and *finally,* can tell you when something happens.

Directions Read the story. Then follow the directions below.

Cass began playing the trumpet in second grade. Now she is in fifth grade and old enough to go to music camp. In the spring, she and her mom applied to the camp. A month ago, she got a letter saying she was accepted. Cass was very excited and could not believe her good luck.

When she got the letter, she also got a list of items she would need at camp. She began to gather these things. First, she bought supplies such as toothpaste and soap. Then Mom took her shopping to get new shorts and tops. She got new sneakers too. Mom helped Cass pack her bags, checking that everything on the list was put in the bags.

Today is the day Cass leaves for camp. Mom is handing the bus driver Cass's bags as Cass boards the bus. Soon Cass will be on her way to camp.

Directions Put the following events from the story in the correct sequence, or time order. Write a number on each line to show the order. For example, write **1** to show which event happened first.

_**3**_ **1.** Cass got a list of things to bring to camp.

_**5**_ **2.** Mom handed the bus driver Cass's bags.

_**2**_ **3.** Cass applied to go to music camp.

_**1**_ **4.** Cass began playing the trumpet.

_**4**_ **5.** Cass and Mom went shopping.

Home Activity This page helps your child identify the sequence of events in a story. Work through the items with your child. Read another story with your child. Ask your child to tell what happened first, next, and last.

Name_____

Writing

Think about animals you've seen or read about. Which one could you keep as a pet? A small one or a large one? A tame one or a wild one? A cute one or a frightening one? How would you take care of it?

Directions: Write the name of an animal you'd like to have as a pet.

1. Name of animal: _____

Now answer the questions below to help you describe the animal. If you need more information, use an encyclopedia or the Internet.

2. What would you name your pet? **Answers to questions will vary.**

_____

3. Would you have to be careful with the animal?

_____

4. What needs does the animal have?

_____

5. What does the animal usually eat?

_____

6. Where would you keep the animal? How would you make a bed for it?

_____

On another paper, write about the animal you'd like to have as a pet. Tell why you chose that animal and how you would care for it. Write complete sentences.

Students' papers should name the animals, give reasons for choosing the animals, and tell how to care for them.

Home Activity This page helps your child write about a pet. Make sure your child gives reasons for choosing that animal as a pet and details about how to care for it.

Vocabulary

Directions Write the word from the box that matches each definition.

<u>evolved</u>   **1.** having developed over time

<u>modify</u>   **2.** to change something to make it better or different

<u>architect</u>   **3.** a person who makes plans for buildings

<u>accustomed</u>   **4.** used to; in the habit of

<u>rare</u>   **5.** not often seen or found

<u>lifestyles</u>   **6.** people's ways of life

<u>adjust</u>   **7.** to get used to

Check the Words You Know

__accustomed
__adjust
__architect
__evolved
__lifestyles
__modify
__rare

Directions Fill in the word from the box that fits the meaning of the sentence.

8. This vase is worth a lot because it is very <u>rare</u> .

9. I've grown <u>accustomed</u> to walking my dog right after lunch.

10. After living in Alaska, you <u>adjust</u> to the cold weather.

11. Jane Rabin is the <u>architect</u> who planned this building.

12. The <u>lifestyles</u> of people in big cities may differ from those of people in small towns.

Write a Paragraph

On a separate paper, write a paragraph about what it would be like to move to a different place. Tell how you would adjust to your new home.

Home Activity This page helps your child read and write vocabulary words. Work through the items with your child. Have your child read the paragraph he or she wrote about adjusting to a new home.

Name_____

Diphthongs *ou* and *ow*

Directions Circle the word with the vowel sound as in *out* or *now*.
Then write the word on the line.

compound   **1.** The word *shipwreck* is a ((compound)/complex) word.

flowers   **2.** Kristen received a beautiful bunch of
(rosebuds/(flowers)).

around   **3.** A fence goes completely (along/(around)) the yard.

crowded   **4.** After the game, everyone ((crowded)/surged) onto the
playing field.

discount   **5.** You will get a (rebate/(discount)) if you buy two or
more T-shirts.

tower   **6.** The builders have almost finished the new
((tower)/skyscraper).

encountered   **7.** The hikers were surprised when they
((encountered)/met) a deer on the path.

shower   **8.** The rain (storm/(shower)) delayed the game only a
short time.

Directions In each row, circle the word that contains the vowel sound
as in *out* or *now*. Write that word on the line.

9. **drowsy**   doodle   (drowsy)   drooped

10. **county**   airport   village   (county)

11. **power**   (power)   prove   prop

12. **aloud**   (aloud)   undone   bother

Home Activity This page practices words with the vowel combinations *ou* as in *out* and *ow* as in *now*.
Work through the items with your child. Say these words: *surround, abound, powder, dowdy.* Help your child
give the meanings of the words and use them in sentences.

Name_____

Main Idea

- The **main idea** is what a passage is all about.
- **Details** are small pieces of information that tell about the main idea.

Directions Read the story. Then follow the directions below.

> **D**id you know you can eat some seeds? Pop a ripe berry in your mouth. You are eating its seeds as well as the berry. Berries have tiny seeds. They can get stuck in your teeth! You can eat bigger seeds too. The beans and peas you eat are seeds. So too is the corn you eat off the cob. Other seeds you do not eat. An apple has small seeds that you don't eat. Cherries have bigger seeds. They are called stones. Peaches have big seeds called pits. Stones and pits are hard and should not be eaten. Biting down on them is a bad idea. You could break your teeth!

Directions Write the main idea on the line by "Main Idea." Then identify four details from the story that support the main idea. Write those on the lines under "Details."

Main Idea
1. **People eat some seeds, but not others.**

Details **Accept any four of the following details:**
2. **You can eat the seeds of berries. Peas and beans are seeds people eat.**
3. **If you eat corn on the cob, you are eating seeds.**
4. **People do not eat apple seeds.**
5. **People do not eat cherry stones. People do not eat peach pits.**

© Pearson Education E

Home Activity This page allows your child to identify the main idea and details in a passage. Work through the items with your child. Then read a short article or story with your child and have him or her identify the main idea and supporting details.

Name_____

Writing

Use your imagination to think about how things will be in twenty years. What will your home or school be like?

Directions: Answer the questions. You can use words from the box to help you write.

1. Think of something in your house today that you use a lot. Write its name on the line.

touchscreen	hover
wireless	movable
soundless	display
incredible	remote
computer	easy-to-use
light panel	

Possible response: television

2. How do you think it will change? Write what you think it will be like in twenty years.

It may respond to voice commands in the future.

3. Think of something in your school today. Write its name on the line.

Possible response: books

4. How do you think it will change in twenty years?

Paper books may be replaced by audio books.

On another paper, write about what your school or house will be like in twenty years. Use words and ideas from this page.

Home Activity This page helps your child write a description of the home or the school of the future. Work through the page with your child. Have your child read the description aloud.

Name_____

Vocabulary

Directions Choose the word from the box that matches each definition. Write the word on the line.

__motivation__   **1.** reason for acting

__balanced__   **2.** steady; changing little

__discipline__   **3.** training for the mind and self-control

__principles__   **4.** rules of action or conduct

__exercise__   **5.** use of the body for its own good

__diet__   **6.** all the things you eat and drink

__nutrition__   **7.** food

> **Check the Words You Know**
>
> __balanced
> __diet
> __discipline
> __exercise
> __motivation
> __nutrition
> __principles

Directions Circle the word at the end of each sentence that fits the meaning. Then write the word on the line to complete the sentence.

8. My __motivation__ to finish this book is finding out how the story ends. (motivation) nutrition

9. Dina takes a __balanced__ approach to work and play. principles, (balanced)

10. It takes __discipline__ to do homework before playing games on the computer. diet, (discipline)

11. Proper __nutrition__ depends on a balanced diet. exercise, (nutrition)

12. Both swimming and running are good forms of __exercise__ . (exercise) principles

Home Activity This page helps your child read and write vocabulary words. Work through the items with your child. Then have your child tell what the vocabulary words in his or her journal entry mean.

© Pearson Education E

Suffixes -al, -ial, -ic

Directions Complete the chart. Write the base word and suffix for each given word.

Word	Base Word	Suffix
1. organic	organ	ic
2. official	office	ial
3. microscopic	microscope	ic
4. personal	person	al
5. athletic	athlete	ic

Directions Read each sentence. Circle the suffix in each underlined word. Then write the definition of the word on the line below. **Hint:** Each of these suffixes means "having characteristics of."

6. I needed financ(ial) aid to help pay for college.

having characteristics of finance_____

7. It's fun to watch that acrobat(ic) monkey swing in the tree.

having characteristics of an acrobat_____

8. Both cotton and silk are natur(al) fibers.

having characteristics of nature_____

9. The inventor's experiment(al) car may not be safe to drive.

having characteristics of an experiment_____

10. Opposite magnet(ic) poles attract each other.

having characteristics of a magnet_____

Home Activity This page practices words formed by adding the suffix -al, -ial, or -ic. Work through the items with your child. Ask your child to add one of the suffixes to these words: linguist (linguistic), margin (marginal), commerce (commercial).

Name_____

Draw Conclusions

- A **conclusion** is a decision you make based on what you read and what you know.
- Use **facts** and **details** to help you draw a conclusion.

Directions Read the story. Then follow the directions below.

It was almost 4:00—time for Carl to be home from school. This morning, he had been very excited. "Today's the day!" he cried. Jane knew what her brother meant. It was the day that three students from Carl's school would be picked for the All-State Band. Carl played the trombone in the school band, and he had been practicing hard all year long. He was a very good trombone player.

Just then, Jane heard the door slam. Carl was home. Without saying a word, he walked up the stairs to his bedroom. "Wait, Carl!" Jane cried.

Directions Answer the questions.   **Possible responses given:**

1. Give two details that show that Carl wanted to be selected for All-State Band.

He was excited that morning; he practiced hard all year.

2. What do you expect people to do when they have good news?

Students are likely to say that people usually can't wait to tell

someone good news. They act excited and share the news eagerly.

3. What do you notice about Carl's actions when he comes home?

He doesn't say anything; he goes straight to his bedroom.

4. Use your answers to 1–3 to help you draw a conclusion about the outcome of the story. Write a complete sentence stating your conclusion.

Carl wasn't selected for the All-State Band.

Home Activity This page allows your child to draw conclusions. Work through the items with your child. Ask your child how the story might have ended if Carl had been picked for All-State Band.

Name_____

Writing

The foods you eat and the exercise you get are two important parts of a healthy lifestyle. Think about your lifestyle and the healthful things you do.

Directions Answer the questions about health and your lifestyle.
Possible responses given:

1. What is your favorite healthful breakfast?

cereal and orange juice

2. What is your favorite healthful lunch?

ham, cheese, and lettuce sandwich, apple, milk

3. What are your favorite healthful snacks?

nuts and carrot sticks

4. What is your favorite kind of exercise?

running

5. How many times do you exercise each week? How long?

once a week

6. Who helps you keep up a healthy lifestyle?

my parents

7. What one thing could you do to make your lifestyle healthier than it is now?

exercise more often

On another page, write a paragraph describing what you do to live a healthy lifestyle. Use ideas from your answers to the questions on this page. Write complete sentences in your paragraph.
Paragraphs should reflect students' responses to the questions.

© Pearson Education E

Home Activity This page helps your child describe his or her lifestyle in terms of healthy diet and exercise. Work through the page with your child. Have your child read the paragraph aloud. Discuss what your family can do to make your lifestyles healthier.

Name_____

Vocabulary

Directions Choose the word from the box that best matches each definition. Write the word on the line.

___reenactment___ **1.** the acting out of an event from the past

___historical___ **2.** famous or important in history

___tradition___ **3.** custom or belief handed down from parents to children

___rendezvous___ **4.** planned meeting at a certain time and place

___century___ **5.** 100 years

___re-create___ **6.** to create, or make, once again

___astonish___ **7.** to surprise greatly

Directions Choose a word from the box that fits the meaning of the sentence. Write the word on the line.

8. Because it is held each year, the talent show has become a ___tradition___ at my school.

9. This book is about Ben Franklin and ___historical___ events that took place during his lifetime.

10. A ___century___ ago, most people did not own cars.

11. The official and the news reporter planned a ___rendezvous___ in the park.

12. Her talent never fails to ___astonish___ me.

Home Activity This page helps your child learn to read and write vocabulary words. Have your child write sentences using each of the vocabulary words. Suggest that your child use the topic of the Fourth of July for the sentences.

© Pearson Education **E**

Name_____

Diphthongs *oi* and *oy*

Directions Circle each word that has the same vowel sound as **oy** in **royal.** Then write the word on the line.

__enjoy_____   **1.** I (enjoy) reading a good story.

__annoyed_____   **2.** Karl was (annoyed) by the dog's yelping and barking.

__boycotted_____   **3.** The colonists (boycotted) tea to protest taxes.

__employs_____   **4.** That company (employs) many workers.

Directions Circle each word that has the same vowel sound as **oi** in **oil.** Then write the word on the line.

__poison_____   **5.** You will get a rash if you touch (poison) ivy.

__appointed_____   **6.** The teacher (appointed) Jan team leader.

__avoid_____   **7.** Drivers should try to (avoid) that street while it is being repaved.

__noisy_____   **8.** The (noisy) crowd cheered for the home team.

Directions Circle each word with the same vowel sound as the first word. Then write the word on the line.

__exploit__	**9. broil**	(exploit)	explain	export
__loyal__	**10. boy**	story	(loyal)	only
__turmoil__	**11. coin**	abound	(turmoil)	contain
__oyster__	**12. toy**	(oyster)	yellow	okay

© Pearson Education E

Home Activity This page practices words with the sound of *oi* in *oil* and the sound of *oy* in *royal*. Have your child list other words that have the vowel sound in *oil* and *toy*. Tell your child to underline the letters that stand for the vowel sound in each word.

Name_____

Draw Conclusions

- Active readers **draw conclusions,** or make decisions, based on information in the text and their own knowledge.

- Examine your own **conclusions** as you read. Ask yourself, "Can I support them with details from the text or with facts I already know?"

Directions Read the following story. Then complete the diagram by writing a conclusion and listing details from the story and facts you already know that support your conclusion.

Amy's class went on a field trip. They learned what it was like to go to school in the late 1800s. They spent all day in a one-room schoolhouse. The teacher rang a big bell in the schoolyard to tell them it was time for school to start. They sat on benches. They learned that the same room was used for all the grades. First graders sat in the front row. The last row was for eighth graders. The same teacher taught all eight grades! They wrote on small chalkboards called slates. At recess, they jumped rope and played tag. Amy had fun at the schoolhouse, but she was glad she did not go to school there!

What Can I Conclude?

1. Amy enjoyed her field trip, but she likes today's schools better than the school from long ago.

What Does the Text Say?

2. In the one-room schoolhouse, students sat on benches.

3. All the grades were in the same room and had the same teacher.

4. Students wrote on slates.

What Do I Already Know?

5. Today, students have their own books and schools have playgrounds.

Home Activity This page allows your child to draw conclusions. Work through the page with your child. Then tell your child a story about what school was like when you were a child. Have your child draw a conclusion about your story and support it with details from the story and his or her own school experience.

Name_____

Writing

Most questions begin with the words *Who, What, When, Where, How,* or *Why.*
Every question ends with a question mark.

Directions Think about what you would like to know about life in
the United States during the 1800s. Think about who would have the
answers to your questions. You might want to ask questions of a famous
person from history. Complete each question. Then put a star by the
question you most want to ask. **Students' questions should focus
on activities during the 1800s. They
might ask about the everyday lives of
ordinary people or about important
events in American history. Their
paragraphs should identify an
individual who would have answers
to their questions and the kind of
answers the individual might provide.**

1. Who _____ ?

_____

2. What _____ ?

_____

3. When _____

_____ ?

4. Where _____

_____ ?

5. How _____

_____ ?

6. Why _____

_____ ?

On another sheet of paper, tell the name of the person from the 1800s
that you want to ask a question. Tell a little bit about the person. Tell what
question you want to ask the person and what you think that person's
answer might be.

Home Activity This page helps your child generate ideas for a writing assignment. Work through the page
with your child. Encourage your child to write detailed questions. Be sure the questions require more than a
simple yes-or-no answer.

© Pearson Education E

Name_____

Vocabulary

Directions Choose the word from the box that best matches each definition. Write the word on the line.

__equipment__   **1.** things someone or something is equipped with, such as supplies, for a specific purpose

__locate__   **2.** to find exactly where something is

__orbit__   **3.** to travel around another object in space

__drill__   **4.** the teaching or training of a skill by repeating it over and over

__exploration__   **5.** the act of traveling in unknown places to discover things

__expedition__   **6.** a trip made by a group of people for a specific purpose

__tracking__   **7.** following persons or things by using marks, tracks, or clues they left

Directions Choose a word from the box to match each clue. Write the word on the line.

__expedition__   **8.** This word means the same as a *journey*.

__orbit__   **9.** This word means the same as *revolve*.

__equipment__   **10.** This word means the same as *supplies*.

Home Activity This page helps your child learn to read and write vocabulary words. Work through the page with your child. Have your child use the words in sentences.

© Pearson Education E

Name_____

Common Syllables

Directions Write the word in each sentence that has a common syllable such as **ion, tion, sion,** or **ture.** Then underline the common syllable.

<u>opin<u>ion</u></u>   **1.** What is your opinion of the school play?

<u>sculp<u>ture</u></u>   **2.** We are going to the sculpture park tomorrow.

<u>men<u>tion</u></u>   **3.** Did he mention when the meeting will begin?

<u>ver<u>sion</u></u>   **4.** Which version of the story do you like best?

<u>furni<u>ture</u></u>   **5.** Patty rearranged the furniture in her bedroom.

<u>collec<u>tion</u></u>   **6.** I keep my shell collection in boxes.

<u>explo<u>sion</u></u>   **7.** Did you hear that loud explosion?

<u>crea<u>ture</u></u>   **8.** My sister enjoys all the creature comforts of home.

<u>ero<u>sion</u></u>   **9.** We are learning about wind and water erosion.

<u>compan<u>ion</u></u>   **10.** A dog can make a great companion.

Directions Read the passage. Underline each word that ends in **tion** or **ture.**

> **W**e didn't know how far it was to the next gas <u>station</u>, and our van was almost out of gas. I could <u>picture</u> in my mind being stranded on the road. I had to <u>question</u> why we didn't fill the tank before we left the city. Just then, we saw a sign for a service stop. Whew! Help was only five miles away. In the <u>future</u>, we will make sure we have enough gas before we leave on an <u>adventure</u>!

© Pearson Education E

Home Activity This page practices words that end with the common syllables *ion, tion, sion,* and *ture.* Ask your child to make lists of words ending with these syllables. Then have your child underline the final syllables.

Name_____

Compare and Contrast

- To **compare** and **contrast** means to tell how two or more things are alike and different.

Directions Read the passage. Then complete the diagram to compare and contrast Susan and her sister.

Susan and her sister, Kathleen, do not look like they are related. Wherever they go, they are always asked the same question: "Are you two really sisters?" Susan and Kathleen both have black hair, but Susan's is curly and Kathleen's is very straight. Susan's eyes are blue, but Kathleen's eyes are brown. Also, Susan is almost 10 inches taller than Kathleen. But the sisters both have winning smiles!

Susan

1. curly hair
2. blue eyes
3. almost 10 inches taller

Both

4. black hair
5. smile

Kathleen

6. straight hair
7. brown eyes
8. about 10 inches shorter

© Pearson Education E

Home Activity This page allows your child to compare and contrast information in a story. Help your child compare his or her features with yours.

Name_____

Writing

Think about the stories you read this week. Think about a place you would like to explore.

Directions Fill in the diagram about an exploration. Name a place to explore. Write the name in the middle oval. In the outside ovals, write details about the exploration. Add more ovals to the diagram if you need to.

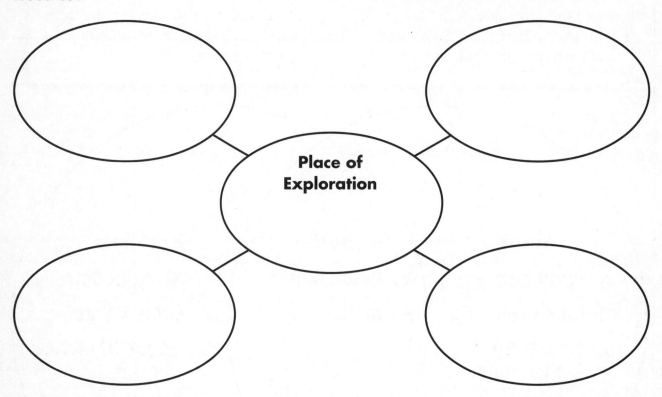

Place of Exploration

On another sheet of paper, write a description of your exploration. Use the information from the diagram in your description.

Students' choices of places to explore may vary. Be sure details are consistent with the place to explore. For example, if the choice is underwater exploration, the student might mention having a command ship, using a submersible, wearing scuba gear, and needing waterproof equipment.

School + Home **Home Activity** This page helps your child gather ideas for writing about an exploration. Work through the page with your child. Encourage your child to add details about the technology needed for the exploration.

Name_____

Vocabulary

Directions Choose the word from the box that best matches each definition. Write the word on the line.

Check the Words You Know

__astronauts
__companions
__consumers
__crew
__products
__program
__shuttle

__consumers__   **1.** people who buy and use goods and services

__program__   **2.** a plan for what is being done

__crew__   **3.** the people who work together on a project

__companions__   **4.** people who go along or spend time with other people

__products__   **5.** things made or grown by people

__astronauts__   **6.** pilots or other members of the crew of a spacecraft

__shuttle__   **7.** a spacecraft that can orbit the Earth, return to it, and be used again

Directions Choose a word from the box to complete each sentence.

8. The airplane's flight __crew__ prepared for departure.

9. The Mars Rover is part of our country's space __program__ .

10. Satellites have been launched from the space __shuttle__ .

11. __Astronauts__ from different countries have spent time working in the space station.

12. Do you know how many __products__ are made from corn?

Home Activity This page helps your child learn to read and write vocabulary words. Work through the page with your child. Have your child write sentences using each of the vocabulary words.

Name_____

Vowel Combinations *oo, ew, ue*

Directions Circle the word in each group that does **not** have the vowel sound in **moon.**

1. poodle (model) monsoon bamboo
2. soon (approach) noodle cartoon
3. spoon shampoo (announce) balloon
4. (spoil) rooster raccoon spool

Directions Circle the word in each sentence that has the same vowel sound as **threw.** Then write the word on the line.

__drew__ 5. My little sister (drew) a picture of our house.

__fewer__ 6. Ms. Samson's class has (fewer) students than Mr. Wong's class.

__newspaper__ 7. Did you read this morning's (newspaper?)

__nephew__ 8. My sister's son is my (nephew.)

Directions Write **ue** to complete each word. Then write the whole word on the line.

__clue__ 9. I don't understand this cl__ue__ to the crossword puzzle!

__continue__ 10. The meeting will contin__ue__ after a short recess.

__value__ 11. Do you know what the val__ue__ of that painting is?

__rescued__ 12. A firefighter resc__ue__d the kitten in the tree.

Home Activity This page practices words with the vowel combinations *oo, ew,* and *ue* that have the vowel sound in *moon.* Work through the page with your child. Ask your child questions that can be answered with words with *oo, ew,* or *ue.* For example, *What do you use to wash your hair? (shampoo)*

© Pearson Education E

Name_____

Draw Conclusions

- A **conclusion** is a decision you make based on what you read and what you know.
- Use **facts** and **details** to help you draw a conclusion.

Directions Read the passage. Then answer the questions that follow.

> Ron and Sam were tired as they sat on the bench, watching the game. The game had been tied after nine innings, and now it was in the second half of the tenth inning. The other team did not score in the first half. Ron and Sam's team already had one runner on base when Jake stepped up to bat. He swung and the ball flew out of the park. Ron and Sam cheered and rushed onto the field.

List four details from the story.   **Possible details include:**

The game had been tied after nine innings, and now it

1. ~~**was in the second half of the tenth inning. The other**~~

2. **team did not score in the first half. Ron and Sam's team**

   already had one runner on base when Jake stepped up

3. ~~**to bat. He swung and the ball flew out of the park. Ron**~~

4. **and Sam cheered and rushed onto the field.**

5. Which of the following is a valid conclusion? Circle your answer. Then explain your reasons.

   Ron and Sam play on different teams.

   (Ron and Sam's team won the game.)

   The game was still tied at the end of the tenth inning.

Jake hit a home run. Ron and Sam would not have cheered and run

onto the field if their team had to play another inning.

Home Activity This page allows your child to read a short passage and draw a conclusion. Read a short story with your child. Then have your child draw a conclusion about one of the characters in the story. Ask your child to identify the details he or she used to help draw a conclusion.

Name_____

Writing

Think about what you know about orbiting Earth in the space shuttle. What is it like traveling to and from the space station? What is it like to live and work in the space station?

Directions Answer each question.

1. How do astronauts get to the space station? **Possible response:**

The space shuttle takes astronauts to the space station.

2. What kind of work do the astronauts do in the space station?

Possible responses: They help build and maintain the space station.

They do scientific experiments.

3. What kinds of food do you think the astronauts eat?

Possible response: They eat packets of dehydrated foods.

4. What do you think the astronauts do to relax?

Possible response: They read or play board games.

5. What do you think would be the easiest part of working in the space station? What would be the hardest part?

Possible response: The easiest part would be doing the work. The

hardest part would be being away from home.

On another sheet of paper, tell whether you would like to live and work at the space station. Give reasons for your choice.

Student's paragraphs should state specific reasons why he or she would or would not want to be an astronaut in the space station.

© Pearson Education E

Home Activity This page helps your child generate ideas for writing about living in the space station. Work through the page with your child. Then have him or her read the paragraph aloud.

Name_____

Vocabulary

Directions Choose the word from the box that best matches each definition. Write the word on the line.

_grotto_____ **1.** a small cave

_chamber_____ **2.** a room

_subterranean____ **3.** under the Earth's surface

_underground_____ **4.** beneath the surface of the ground

_stalactite_____ **5.** a formation hanging from the roof of a cave

_stalagmite_____ **6.** a formation built up on the floor of a cave

_cavern_____ **7.** a large cave

_tunnel_____ **8.** an underground path or road

Check the Words You Know

__cavern
__chamber
__grotto
__stalactite
__stalagmite
__subterranean
__tunnel
__underground

Directions Write a word from the box to match each clue.

_tunnel_____ **9.** I'm like an underground tube you can pass through. What am I?

_stalagmite_____ **10.** I can be found building up on a cave floor. What am I?

_stalactite_____ **11.** I can be found hanging down from a cave ceiling. What am I?

_grotto_____ **12.** I am a cave whose name rhymes with *motto*. What am I?

© Pearson Education E

Home Activity This page helps your child learn to read and write vocabulary words. Work through the page with your child. Ask your child to make a list of other words that start with *sub-* and *under-*. Encourage him or her to use a dictionary.

Name_____

Vowel Sound in *ball:*
a, al, au, aw, augh, ough

Directions Circle the word in each group that has the vowel sound as in **ball**.

1. taken   (recall)   retail   demand
2. sailing   garment   cranked   (walnut)
3. (talking)   alley   remain   yard
4. about   carpool   (alter)   rapid

Directions Circle the word in each sentence that has the same vowel sound as **launch** and **saw.** Then write the word on the line.

__author__   **5.** Dennis knows the (author) of the book we are reading in English class.

__strawberries__   **6.** These ripe (strawberries) taste sweet.

__August__   **7.** My father's birthday is in (August.)

__awkward__   **8.** I sometimes feel (awkward) meeting new people.

Directions Read the passage. Circle each word that has the same vowel sound as **caught** and **thought.**

Mr. Ellis (taught) English in our school for over 20 years. When he retired from teaching, we tried to think of something (thoughtful) to do for him. We (sought) help from his (daughter.) She suggested that we throw a surprise party. We wrote to many of his former students. Lots of them said they would come. On the day of the party, I was (distraught) when Mr. Ellis began to leave the school. But another teacher stopped him and asked for his help in the gym. When they came through the door, everyone shouted "Surprise!" You (ought) to have seen his face. He was really surprised!

© Pearson Education E

School + Home **Home Activity** This page practices words with the vowel sound in *ball* spelled *a, al, au, aw, augh,* and *ough.* Work through the page with your child. Have your child write sentences using words that have the same vowel sound as *ball.*

Name_____

Sequence

- **Sequence** is the order of events in a story.
- Clue words such as *first, next,* and *then* can help you follow the **sequence** of events.

Directions Read the passage. Then complete the diagram below.

Kent and his mother were visiting Washington, D.C. His mom said they could visit Arlington National Cemetery by taking the Metro. Kent was planning a route for them to follow. The College Park station was near their hotel. So, they'd buy their tickets and board the Metro's Green Line at College Park. They would ride the Green Line to the Fort Totten station. Next, they would transfer to the Red Line and ride it to Metro Center. Then they'd transfer to the Blue Line, which would take them across the Potomac River to Alexandria, Virginia. The Arlington Cemetery station was the second stop after the river. Getting back to their hotel would be a snap! They'd just retrace the route.

Sequence of Events

1. Kent's family's trip would start at __the College Park station__ .

↓

2. They would make the first transfer at __the Fort Totten station__ .

↓

3. They would make the next transfer at __Metro Center__ .

↓

4. The Arlington Cemetery station would be the second stop __after__ they crossed the river.

5. On another sheet of paper, describe the route Kent's family will need to follow to return to their hotel. **Blue Line to Metro Center to Red Line, to Fort Totten, Green Line, College Park**

Home Activity This page allows your child to read a short passage and identify the sequence of events. Have your child describe how to travel from your home to school. Encourage your child to use the words *first, next,* and *then* as he or she describes the route.

© Pearson Education E

Name_____

Writing

What do you know about caves? Have you ever been in one? Think about what you know about caves and the people who explore them. Think about what you might see and how you would describe it.

Directions Answer each question.

1. What would you need to take with you to explore a cave?

Possible responses: flashlights, ropes, water

2. What physical features do you think you would see while exploring a cave?

Possible responses: stalactites, stalagmites, rocks, tunnels, and

chambers

3. Do you think you would see any animals? What kinds of animals?

Possible response: You might see insects and bats.

4. What words might an explorer use to describe what he or she sees, feels, smells, or hears in a cave?

Possible responses: colorful, damp, dark, close, open, quiet

On another sheet of paper, write a story about exploring caves. Tell what you would see, feel, smell, touch, and hear in the cave. Use colorful words to help the reader picture what you are describing.
Descriptions should tell about exploring a cave and give details about its contents and size.

Home Activity This page helps your child generate ideas for writing about caves and their explorations. Discuss with your child what it would be like to be in a cave. Have your child describe what someone in a cave can see, feel, smell, touch, and hear.

© Pearson Education E

Vocabulary

Directions Choose the word from the box that matches each
definition. Write the word on the line.

__necessities__   **1.** things that are impossible to
do without

__hardship__   **2.** a condition of living that
causes trouble or pain

__enterprises__   **3.** projects or businesses

__trail__   **4.** a path through woods or
wilderness

__route__   **5.** a road or course for traveling from one place
to another

__claim__   **6.** to ask for or take something as one's own

__journey__   **7.** a trip over a great distance

> **Check the Words
> You Know**
>
> __claim
> __enterprises
> __hardship
> __journey
> __necessities
> __route
> __trail

Directions Circle the word that has the same or nearly the same
meaning as the first word in each group.

8. enterprises	surprises	entries	(projects)
9. hardship	(difficulty)	compass	metal
10. journey	diary	(trip)	business
11. route	(way)	round	source
12. trail	train	(path)	leave

© Pearson Education E

Home Activity This page helps your child learn to read and write vocabulary words. Work through the
page with your child. Discuss the meaning of each word from the vocabulary list. Help your child use each
word in a sentence.

Name_____

Suffixes -ness, -ment, -ity, -ty, -ous

Directions For each word, write the base word and suffix.

	Base Word	**Suffix**
1. sadness	sad	ness
2. equipment	equip	ment
3. prosperity	prosper	ity
4. safety	safe	ty
5. dangerous	danger	ous

Directions Add the suffix to each base word. Write the new word.

6. sick   +   ness   =   sickness

7. excite   +   ment   =   excitement

8. sincere   +   ity   =   sincerity

9. certain   +   ty   =   certainty

10. joy   +   ous   =   joyous

Directions Choose a word from the box that fits each definition. Write the word on the line.

____unity____ **11.** the condition of being united

__authenticity__ **12.** the state of being authentic

____famous____ **13.** having the quality of fame

___happiness___ **14.** the condition of being happy

__contentment__ **15.** the state of being content

> authenticity
> contentment
> famous
> happiness
> unity

© Pearson Education E

Home Activity This page practices words that end with the suffixes -ness, -ment, -ity, -ty, and -ous. These suffixes mean "state," "condition," or "quality." Work through the page with your child. Ask your child to write definitions for the words in items 6–10. Then ask them to write sentences using the words.

Name_____

Main Idea

- The **main idea** is the most important idea in the selection.
- **Details** are small pieces of information that tell more about the main idea.
- If the author does not state the **main idea,** then the reader must use the details to figure it out.

Directions Read the following passage. Then complete the diagram below. **Possible responses are given.**

The "Gold Vault" of the United States Treasury is located at Fort Knox, Kentucky. It opened in 1937. Today, it stores over 145 million ounces of gold that belong to the United States government. The total value of the gold is over six billion dollars! In the past, the vault has also stored other types of national treasures. During World War II, the Declaration of Independence and the U.S. Constitution were sent to the "Gold Vault" for safekeeping. It has also stored the originals of Lincoln's famous Gettysburg Address and important items for other governments. No visitors are permitted inside!

Main Idea
1. **The "Gold Vault" at Fort Knox is very safe.**

Details
2. **It stores gold worth over six billion dollars.**

3. **It has been used to store national treasures.**

4. **It has been used to store important items for other countries.**

5. **No visitors are permitted.**

© Pearson Education E

Home Activity This page allows your child to identify the main idea and supporting details of a passage. Work together to identify the main idea and supporting details of individual paragraphs in a newspaper article.

Name_____

Writing

Think about going west to California in search of gold during the 1849 Gold Rush. What kind of people would have left home to look for gold? Was it something everyone would do? Would you have wanted to go west in search of gold?

Directions Circle the words below that might be used to describe what it would be like to leave home and go to California in search of gold.

| frightening | awesome | dangerous | scary | fun |
| adventuresome | exciting | stressful | risky | new |

Directions Use your ideas to fill in the word web. Pretend you are living in 1849. Would you go west? If so, fill in the middle oval with "I'd go west." Would you stay at home? If so, fill in the middle oval with "I'd stay home." Then write your reasons in the outer ovals.

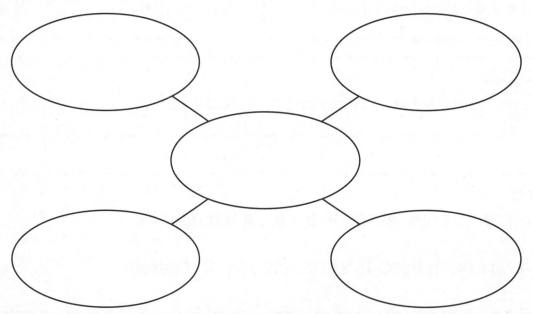

On another sheet of paper answer the question: If you lived in 1849, would you have gone west to seek gold? Write at least two reasons for your answer.

Possible response: I would go west because it would be exciting to pan for gold. If I struck it rich, I could take care of my whole family.

Home Activity This page helps your child gather ideas for answering the question: If you lived in 1849, would you have gone west to seek gold? Discuss your child's answer. Help him or her understand why different people make different decisions.

© Pearson Education E

Name_____

Vocabulary

Directions Choose the word from the box that best fits the meaning of the sentence. Write the word on the line.

Check the Words You Know

__disappointed
__encountered
__hitch
__misfortune
__predict
__solution
__surprise

1. Val's dad did not know about the party planned as a big __**surprise**__ for him.

2. The __**misfortune**__ of losing his wallet was the beginning of Anthony's unlucky day.

3. Maria felt __**disappointed**__ when she didn't win the spelling bee.

4. I was able to make my connecting flight without a single __**hitch**__ .

5. Nora and Tim __**encountered**__ a snake on their wetlands walk.

6. I __**predict**__ Erin will win the election for class president.

7. I can help you find a __**solution**__ to the problem.

Directions Choose the word from the box that best matches each clue. Write the word on the line.

__**encountered**__ 8. This means about the same as "met unexpectedly."

__**solution**__ 9. This is the answer to a problem.

__**predict**__ 10. You do this when you tell what you think will happen next in a story.

__**misfortune**__ 11. This word means "bad luck."

__**disappointed**__ 12. You could be this if your team lost a baseball game.

© Pearson Education E

Home Activity This page helps your child read and write vocabulary words. Work through the items with your child. Then ask your child to use each vocabulary word in a sentence.

Prefixes *pre-, mid-, post-*

Directions Add the prefix **pre-**, **mid-**, or **post-** to each base word.
Write the new word on the line.

1. mid + point = __midpoint__

2. pre + view = __preview__

3. post + date = __postdate__

4. mid + term = __midterm__

5. mid + afternoon = __midafternoon__

6. pre + recorded = __prerecorded__

7. pre + shrunk = __preshrunk__

Directions Add the prefix **pre-**, **mid-**, or **post-** to the base word in
( ) to complete each sentence. Then write the word on the line.

__postscript__   **8.** I forgot to write something, so I'll add a (script).

__pregame__   **9.** The (game) celebration in the park began an
                       hour before the beginning of the game.

__midweek__   **10.** I scheduled a (week) appointment for Wednesday
                       afternoon.

__posttest__   **11.** After completing the unit, we took a (test) to find
                       out what we learned.

__preheat__   **12.** Dad said to (heat) the oven to 350 degrees.

© Pearson Education E

School + Home   **Home Activity** This page practices words containing the prefixes *pre-*, *mid-*, and *post-*. Work through the
items with your child. Ask your child to think of new words with these prefixes.

Name_____

Draw Conclusions

- A **conclusion** is a decision you reach based on what you read and what you know.
- Use **facts** and **details** to help you reach a conclusion.

Directions Read the following passage. Then complete the diagram below. **Possible responses are given.**

Nikki wanted Aunt Alma to learn how to use a computer. If she did that, she'd be able to send Nikki e-mail. They could have a chat every day.

Nikki talked to Mom about it. "I think Aunt Alma is afraid of using computers," said Nikki. "I think she should take lessons."

Mom thought that was a great idea and talked to Aunt Alma about taking a class at the senior center. She thought Aunt Alma would learn quickly.

A week later, Nikki turned on her computer. Mom saw a smile spread across Nikki's face and asked what was up. "I've got mail from someone very special!" said Nikki.

| **Tell what you know about e-mail.** 1. **It's quick and easy— much faster than sending a letter.** | **Give a story detail.** 2. Nikki wanted **Aunt Alma to learn how to use a computer to send and receive e-mail.** | **Give a story detail.** 3. Mom said **that Aunt Alma would learn quickly.** | **Give a story detail.** 4. When Nikki turned on her computer, **she smiled and said she had mail from someone special.** |

Give a conclusion.
5. **Aunt Alma learned how to use the computer and sent Nikki an e-mail message.**

Home Activity This page helps your child draw a conclusion from details in a story. Work through the items with your child. After your child has completed the page, ask how the conclusion would have been different if Nikki had seemed sad at the end.

Name_____

Writing

Think about a problem that you or a friend might have. Think about ways of solving the problem. Which solution is best? Describe the problem and solution.

Directions Identify a problem that needs to be solved. Identify possible ways to solve the problem. Write your answers in the chart.

Problem	1. **Responses will vary but chart should identify a problem, such as missing the school bus this morning**
Possible Solutions	2. **and list possible solutions to the problem.**

Now answer the following questions.

3. What was the problem? Why is it a problem?

Responses will vary but should give specific reasons why something

is a problem.

4. What do you think is the best solution? Tell why it is the best way to solve the problem.

Responses will vary but should identify the best solution, explaining

why it is the best one.

On another sheet of paper, write a description of the problem and solution. Use the chart and answers to the questions in the description. Be sure to check your spelling.

Home Activity This page helps your child write about a problem and solution. Work through the page with your child. Have your child read the description aloud.

Name_____

Vocabulary

Directions Choose the word from the box that matches each definition. Write the word on the line.

___thrive___   **1.** to grow strong

___wonder___   **2.** an amazing thing to see

___depend___   **3.** to count on for help

___acres___   **4.** pieces of land of a
                                particular size

___promote___   **5.** to spur, push, or persuade

___preserve___   **6.** to save

___contaminates___ **7.** makes something impure or dirty

Directions Choose a word from the box that best completes each sentence. Write the word on the line.

8. Our garden store is using ads to ___promote___ garden plants this spring.

9. I think it's important to protect and ___preserve___ forests and open spaces for people's long-term enjoyment.

10. A plant will ___thrive___ if it gets plenty of sun, water, and nutrients from the soil.

11. You can always ___depend___ on me when you need help.

12. Cara thinks that the Grand Canyon is a ___wonder___ of nature.

Home Activity This page helps your child read and write vocabulary words. Work through the items with your child. Then have your child write a letter to a government official in your community. Explain that you would like to see more flowers and trees planted. Suggest that your child use the vocabulary words in the letter.

Name_____

Vowels *oo* in *foot*, *u* in *put*

Directions Circle each word that contains the vowel sound in **foot** and **put.** Then write the words in the correct column below.

1. You can (unhook) the gate latch by (pulling) it up.

2. All the travelers (fully) (understood) that they had to be at the airport two hours before their flight.

3. Flowering (bushes) surround our (neighborhood) park.

4. Lee said he'd build (wooden) (bookcases).

5. To straighten the (crooked) picture, I (pushed) one side up.

6. The (butcher) explained how to prepare the turkey for (cooking).

oo as in **foot**	**u** as in **put**
7. <u>unhook</u>	14. <u>pulling</u>
8. <u>understood</u>	15. <u>fully</u>
9. <u>neighborhood</u>	16. <u>bushes</u>
10. <u>wooden</u>	17. <u>pushed</u>
11. <u>bookcases</u>	18. <u>butcher</u>
12. <u>crooked</u>	**Accept *u* words in any order.**
13. <u>cooking</u>	

Accept *oo* words in any order.

School + Home **Home Activity** This page practices words with the vowels *oo* as in *foot* and *u* as in *put*. Work through the items with your child. Ask your child to say and spell the words.

Name_____

Main Idea

- The **main idea** is what a passage is all about.
- **Details** are small pieces of information that tell about the main idea.

Directions Read the passage. Then complete the diagram by writing the main idea and four details that support it. Write a complete sentence for the main idea. Write words or phrases for the details.

Many foods we eat are actually the seeds of plants. Do you like sunflower seeds or pumpkin seeds for a snack? It's easy to see that they are seeds. You eat other seeds too. Maybe you have had a bread roll with sesame seeds on it.

Do you like rice? When you eat rice, you are eating the seeds of the rice plant. Corn, peas, and all kinds of beans are seeds too. And chocolate is made from the seeds of a plant grown in hot, wet climates.

Possible responses are given.

> **2. sunflower seeds, pumpkin seeds, sesame seeds**

> **3. rice, corn, peas**

Supporting Details

> **Main Idea**
> **1. Many foods are seeds of plants.**

Supporting Details

> **4. all kinds of beans**

> **5. chocolate**

Home Activity This page helps your child identify the main idea and supporting details in a passage. Work through the items with your child. Prompt your child to imagine rewriting the story to be about foods that come from stems or roots instead of seeds. Help him or her identify a main idea and some details.

© Pearson Education E

Name_____

Writing

Conserving means using things wisely without wasting them. *Recycling* means using things again rather than throwing them away. Think about what may happen to our Earth if no one conserves or recycles.

Directions Circle any terms from the box that you can use to discuss conserving and recycling. Then answer the questions.

planet	environment	energy
shortage	pollution	air
water	breathe	resources
recycle	conserve	clean up
electricity	air conditioner	reuse

What might happen if people forget about conserving? Write two ideas.

1. <u>Responses will vary but should include two ideas about the</u>

   <u>consequences of failing to conserve, such as running out</u>

2. <u>of resources.</u>

   _____

What might happen if people do not recycle? Write two ideas.

3. <u>Responses will vary but should include two ideas about the</u>

   <u>consequences of failing to recycle, such as overflowing landfills.</u>

4. _____

   _____

On another sheet of paper, write a paragraph to explain why conserving and recycling are important. Use ideas from your answers to the questions on this page. **Paragraphs should explain the importance of conserving and recycling to the environment.**

Home Activity This page helps your child generate ideas about the importance of conserving and recycling. Work through the page with your child. Then have your child list what your family can do to conserve or recycle.

© Pearson Education E

Vocabulary

Directions Choose the word from the box that best completes each sentence. Write the word on the line.

1. Let's __exchange__ phone numbers before we leave.

2. "Pay attention," the teacher said. "This lesson is __important__ ."

3. Would this old clock be __worth__ a lot at the flea market?

4. If I had to put a __monetary__ value on it, I'd say fifty dollars.

5. This is the most __valuable__ gem in the whole collection.

6. A country's __currency__ is the bills and coins used as money.

7. They had no money, so they decided to __barter__ goods.

> **Check the Words You Know**
>
> __barter
> __currency
> __exchange
> __important
> __monetary
> __valuable
> __worth

Directions Choose the word from the box that best completes each sentence. Write the word on the line.

People in the colony decided how much each item was

8. __worth__ . When trading, a basket weaver might

9. __barter (or exchange)__ one basket for a sack of corn. Today, we might think the basket is much more 10. __valuable__ than that. We might put a high 11. __monetary__ value on it—for example, $200. And we might pay for it with 12. __currency__ or credit cards.

Write a Letter

On a separate paper, write a letter to the owner of a store that sells old things. Write about something old you have that you'd like to sell.

Home Activity This page helps your child read and write vocabulary words. Work through the items with your child. Then have your child tell you the meaning of the vocabulary words in his or her letter.

Long *i*: -ind, -ild; Long *o*: -ost, -old

Directions Circle the word in each sentence that has the **long i** sound as in **find** and **child**. Then write the word on the line.

wildly **1.** The crowd waved (wildly) to the movie stars entering the theater.

remind **2.** Please (remind) me to return the books.

childhood **3.** Mom said her scrapbook was filled with (childhood) treasures.

binder **4.** I have to buy a three-ring (binder) for school.

hind **5.** One of our dog's tricks is standing on its (hind) legs and walking.

Directions Circle the word in each sentence that has the **long o** sound as **most** and **gold**. Then write the word on the line.

oldest **6.** Great-uncle Jake is the (oldest) person in my family.

almost **7.** I (almost) missed the bus this morning when I left the house late.

golden **8.** Janet received a (golden) medal for winning the speech contest.

folding **9.** We need to pick up some (folding) chairs for the party on Friday.

household **10.** You can remove that stain with any (household) cleaner.

Home Activity This page practices words with long *i* as in *find* and *wild* and long *o* as in *most* and *hold*. Work through the items with your child. Ask your child to say and spell *mildly, kindness, folded,* and *postcard.*

© Pearson Education E

Name_____

Compare and Contrast

- To **compare** and **contrast** means to tell how two or more things are alike and different.

Directions Read the story. Then answer the questions that follow.

Professor Post and Professor Gold were in a race. Each one was trying to build the world's first time machine. A time machine was supposed to take someone from the present back to the past. Professor Post developed the Post formula for time travel and made her machine out of plastic. She also used solar power for energy. Professor Gold thought the Post formula for time travel was wrong, so he developed the Gold formula. He built his machine out of metal and used big batteries for power. In the end, however, the professors did have one thing in common. Neither of their time machines worked!

1. How were Professor Post's and Professor Gold's time machines alike?

They both didn't work.

How were the two professors' time machines different? Answer this question by completing the chart.

Professor Post's Machine	Professor Gold's Machine
2. **Accept two responses: used Post formula for time travel; made out of plastic;** **3.** **used solar power**	**4.** **Accept two responses: used Gold formula for time travel; made out of** **5.** **metal; used big batteries for power**

© Pearson Education E

Home Activity This page helps your child compare and contrast elements of a story. Work through the page together. Then prompt your child to think of two different but enjoyable games. Have him or her explain one way they are alike and one way they are different.

Name_____

Writing

Think about the things you value the most. How could you describe their value? What price would you put on them?

Directions Choose three things that have great value to you. They may be ideas, objects, or people. Write them on the lines A, B, and C below. Then answer the questions. **Responses will vary, but students should list three things they value on lines A, B, and C.**

1. A. _____

   B. _____

   C. _____

2. Rate your three things on a scale from 1 to 10. The thing you value the most should be highest on the scale. Write the letters A, B, and C above the scale to show how you rate them.

Students should write *A*, *B*, and *C* above the scale to rate the items.

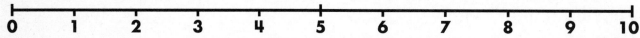

0   1   2   3   4   5   6   7   8   9   10

3. What did you rate the highest?

Students should identify the item they rated highest.

4. Why do you value it the most?

Responses will vary, but students' explanations should be well

reasoned and clear.

_____

On another sheet of paper, write a paragraph explaining what you value and why. Use your answers on this page for ideas.

© Pearson Education E

School + Home **Home Activity** This page helps your child write about something he or she values highly. Work through the page with your child. Then have your child read his or her paragraph aloud.

Name_____

Vocabulary

Directions Circle the word that completes each sentence. Then write the word on the line.

1. Our tour group has three island __**destinations**__ to visit on this trip.

   passengers   (destinations)

2. One of Dru and May's favorite __**conveyances**__ is a bicycle built for two.

   (conveyances)   freight

3. __**Travel**__ to other countries is fun, but it can be tiring too.

   Conveyance   (Travel)

4. This __**transcontinental**__ train goes from coast to coast.

   conveyance   (transcontinental)

5. Most trucks carry __**freight**__ , not passengers.

   travel   (freight)

6. Trains and trucks are two forms of __**transportation**__ .

   (transportation)   freight

7. "We only have seats for two more __**passengers**__ ," said the bus driver.

   destinations   (passengers)

Write a Description

On a separate sheet of paper, write about an interesting place you have visited. Describe the things you saw and heard.

Answers will vary.

Home Activity This page helps your child read and write vocabulary words. Work through the items with your child. Then have your child read his or her description.

© Pearson Education E

Syllables V/V

Directions In each sentence, circle the word with two vowels together where each vowel has a separate sound, as in *piano*. Then write the word on the line.

__lion__   **1.** We saw a (lion) at the zoo yesterday.

__patio__   **2.** Let's have lunch on the (patio.)

__ideas__   **3.** We can brainstorm some new (ideas.)

__rodeo__   **4.** Jill will ride a horse in the (rodeo.)

__diet__   **5.** Dad is on a (diet) to lose some weight.

__stereo__   **6.** Your (stereo) is too loud!

__poetry__   **7.** I like (poetry) written by Robert Frost.

__video__   **8.** We've lost the (video) on our TV.

Directions For the words below, write each syllable on the lines to show how the word is pronounced.

9. create   __cre__   __ate__

10. meander   __me__   __an__   __der__

11. react   __re__   __act__

12. violin   __vi__   __o__   __lin__

13. science   __sci__   __ence__

14. influence   __in__   __flu__   __ence__

15. triumph   __tri__   __umph__

Home Activity This page practices words with two vowels together that have two distinct vowel sounds as in *lion* or *patio*. Work through the items with your child. Ask your child to say and spell *pioneer, reaction,* and *angiogram.*

© Pearson Education E

Name_____

Main Idea and Supporting Details

- The **main idea** is the most important idea in a passage. It tells what the passage is about. Sometimes the main idea is not stated. You use supporting details to help name the main idea.

- **Supporting details** are small pieces of information that tell about the main idea.

Directions Read the passage. Then answer the questions below.

D o you live in a rainy place? Or do you live where it is usually dry? The amount of rain that falls in a year is very different from place to place on Earth. Some deserts, for example, have less than one inch of rainfall in a whole year! Very few living things can make their homes in such dry places.

On the other hand, there are places that receive as much as 450 inches of rainfall in a year. In the United States, Alaska is the rainiest place. Some parts of that state receive more than 200 inches of rain in a year. Places such as these have a different problem: They are soggy all the time!

Possible responses are given.

1. Most of the details have something to do with rainfall. What is the whole passage about?

<u>**rainfall in different places**</u>

Give details about rainfall. Write them on the lines below.

2. <u>**Some deserts receive less than one inch of rainfall in a year.**</u>

<u>**Some places receive as much as 450 inches of rainfall in a year.**</u>

<u>**Parts of Alaska receive more than 200 inches of rainfall a year.**</u>

3. Think about all the details in the passage. Think of what the passage is about. In a complete sentence, write the main idea.

<u>**The amount of rain that falls in a year is very different from place to**</u>

<u>**place on Earth.**</u>

Home Activity This page helps your child identify the main idea and supporting details in a passage. Work through the items with your child. Ask your child to do some research to find details about rain to add to the passage.

Name_____

Writing

People have always needed different ways to get around. What way could you design? Use your imagination!

---

smooth	rapid	zip	scenic	cross-crountry
journey	wheels	easy	zoom	pleasant

Directions Circle any words from the box that you might use. Write other words you can use in your design for a dream vehicle.

1. Responses will vary, but students should write vehicle-related terms.

Now answer the questions.

2. What will be the main use of your vehicle? For example, some vehicles are for recreation while others are for moving things.

Responses will vary, but students should offer a brief description of

how their vehicles will be used.

3. What part of your design will capture people's attention the most? Describe that part.

Responses will vary, but students should incorporate attention-

getting features into their designs.

On another sheet of paper, write a description of your design for a dream vehicle. The design should make your friends want to see a model or picture. Draw a picture if you'd like. Label the picture and make sure all your writing is correctly spelled and punctuated.

© Pearson Education E

Home Activity This page helps your child create a design for a dream vehicle. Work through the page with your child. Have your child describe his or her design, and encourage him or her to make changes as desired.

Name_____

Vocabulary

Directions Circle the one or two words that can have the given meaning. Then write each word on a line to complete the sentence.

1. to get someone to do something or believe something

   commercial   (convince)   (persuade)

If you __**persuade**__ someone to do something, you __**convince**__ them to do it.

2. paid advertising message that tells about a product or service

   (advertisement)   (commercials)   control

The 30-second __**commercials**__ on television are an __**advertisement**__ for a home computer.

3. to have power over

   (control)   gullible   (influence)

If you can __**control**__ what someone thinks, you can __**influence**__ his or her actions.

4. easily deceived or cheated

   advertisement   (gullible)   persuade

Only a very __**gullible**__ person would believe that the events in that story really happened.

> **Check the Words You Know**
>
> __advertisement
> __commercials
> __control
> __convince
> __gullible
> __influence
> __persuade

Write a Product Description

On a separate sheet of paper, write a description of a product you like to use. Read and revise what you have written. Then think of some words, phrases, or sentences to add that may make other people want to buy the product. Use as many vocabulary words as you can.

Home Activity This page helps your child read and write vocabulary words. Work through the items with your child. Have your child read his or her product description.

© Pearson Education E

Name_____

Related Words

Directions Choose a word from the box to complete the sentence. Write that word on the line. (**Hint:** The word you choose will be related to another word in the sentence.)

athletic
clothing
decision
energetic
relaxation
repetition
signal

1. I don't have much energy today, but I hope I'll be more __energetic__ tomorrow.

2. __Relaxation__ is important to good health, so you must learn to relax.

3. I like my __clothing__ to be made of cotton cloth.

4. A traffic __signal__ would be much better than a stop sign at that intersection.

5. Decide what you want to do, and I'll help you carry out your __decision__ .

6. How many athletes have signed up for this __athletic__ competition?

7. __Repetition__ always helps, so repeat the activity several times.

Directions Choose the word that best matches each clue. Write the word on the line.

8. statement of the meaning (define, definition) __definition__

9. skilled or talented in music (musical, musician) __musical__

10. friendly and cheerful (please, pleasant) __pleasant__

11. a skill (able, ability) __ability__

12. your name written by you (signature, sign) __signature__

13. an aunt or an uncle (relative, relate) __relative__

14. something you make (create, creation) __creation__

© Pearson Education E

Home Activity This page practices related words. Work through the items with your child. Prompt your child to think of related words that could be paired with *meaning, baker,* and *decoration (mean, bake, decorate).*

Name_____

Sequence

- **Sequence** is the order in which things happen in a story.
- **Clue words,** such as *when, first, then, after,* and *finally,* can tell you when something happens.

Directions Read the story. Then follow the directions below.

When we went camping, Jen and I helped Mom and Dad put up the tent. First, we all picked up sticks and stones to make the ground smooth. Then Mom stretched out the material on the ground. She and Dad pounded a stake into the ground at each corner of the tent. Jen and I helped do some of the hammering. After that, we each tied a stake to a ring in one of the tent corners. Dad helped me with my corner. Finally, Mom and Dad stood the center pole up in the inside middle of the tent. Now the tent was ready for use!

Directions Based on the story, write instructions for putting up a tent. Use the phrases in the box to help you. Put them in the correct order, and write complete sentences on the lines.
Wording will vary.

> **putting up the center pole**
> **tying stakes to tent corners**
> **laying material on the ground**
> **driving stakes into the ground**
> **preparing the ground**

Instructions for Putting Up a Tent

1. **First, prepare the ground by picking up sticks and stones.**

2. **Then lay the tent material out on the ground.**

3. **Next, drive stakes into the ground at the corners of the tent.**

4. **After that, tie each stake to the nearest tent corner.**

5. **Finally, put up the center pole in the inside middle of the tent.**

Home Activity This page helps your child identify sequence in the description of a task. Work through the items with your child. Then find a set of instructions, such as directions for cooking a frozen dinner. Read the steps out of order, and challenge your child to tell what the proper order should be.

© Pearson Education E

Name_____

Writing

Think about a vegetable or fruit you like to eat. How could you describe it? Could you write an advertisement that would make others want to try it?

Directions Circle any words from the box that you might use in your advertisement. You can use these words in the web to help describe the fruit or vegetable you choose. Complete the web. **Webs will vary, but students should choose a specific fruit or vegetable, describe its taste and texture, identify dishes in which it is used, and name the favorite way to eat the food.**

delicious	flavor
rich	crunchy
smooth	aroma
sour	sweet
texture	spicy
taste	salty
buds	intense

Texture of the Food

Taste of the Food

Fruit or Vegetable

Dishes Using the Food

Favorite Way to Serve Food

© Pearson Education E

Create an advertisement for your favorite food. Make the food seem so tasty that others will want to try it. Use words and ideas from this page. Include your own art, too. **The advertisements should use words and pictures to persuade readers to try the fruit or vegetable.**

Home Activity This page helps your child create an advertisement. Work through the page with your child. Encourage your child to share the ad with you. Brainstorm some ideas with your child to improve the ad and make the fruit or vegetable seem even more delicious.

Name _____

Reading Log

Date	What is the title?	Who is the author?	What did you think of it?

Name _____

Reading Log

Date	What is the title?	Who is the author?	What did you think of it?

Name _____

Reading Log

Date	What is the title?	Who is the author?	What did you think of it?

Name _____

Reading Log

Date	What is the title?	Who is the author?	What did you think of it?